P9-DWT-269

DISCARDED

MEDICAL DIAGNOSIS

GENERAL EDITORS

Dale C. Garell, M.D.
Medical Director, California Children Services, Department of Health Services,
    County of Los Angeles
Associate Dean for Curriculum; Clinical Professor, Department of Pediatrics &
    Family Medicine, University of Southern California School of Medicine
Former President, Society for Adolescent Medicine

Solomon H. Snyder, M.D.
Distinguished Service Professor of Neuroscience, Pharmacology, and Psychiatry,
    Johns Hopkins University School of Medicine
Former President, Society for Neuroscience
Albert Lasker Award in Medical Research, 1978

CONSULTING EDITORS

Robert W. Blum, M.D., Ph.D.
Professor and Director, Division of General Pediatrics and Adolescent Health,
    University of Minnesota

Charles E. Irwin, Jr., M.D.
Professor of Pediatrics; Director, Division of Adolescent Medicine, University of
    California, San Francisco

Lloyd J. Kolbe, Ph.D.
Director of the Division of Adolescent and School Health, Center for Chronic
    Disease Prevention and Health Promotion, Centers for Disease Control

Jordan J. Popkin
Former Director, Division of Federal Employee Occupational Health, U.S. Public
    Health Service Region I

Joseph L. Rauh, M.D.
Professor of Pediatrics and Medicine, Adolescent Medicine, Children's Hospital
    Medical Center, Cincinnati
Former President, Society for Adolescent Medicine

THE ENCYCLOPEDIA OF
HEALTH

MEDICAL DISORDERS
AND THEIR TREATMENT

Dale C. Garell, M.D. • General Editor

MEDICAL
DIAGNOSIS

Don Nardo

Introduction by C. Everett Koop, M.D., Sc.D.
former Surgeon General, U. S. Public Health Service

CHELSEA HOUSE PUBLISHERS

New York • Philadelphia

The goal of the ENCYCLOPEDIA OF HEALTH *is to provide general information in the ever-changing areas of physiology, psychology, and related medical issues. The titles in this series are not intended to take the place of the professional advice of a physician or other health care professional.*

CHELSEA HOUSE PUBLISHERS
EDITOR-IN-CHIEF   Remmel Nunn
MANAGING EDITOR   Karyn Gullen Browne
COPY CHIEF   Mark Rifkin
PICTURE EDITOR   Adrian G. Allen
ART DIRECTOR   Maria Epes
ASSISTANT ART DIRECTOR   Howard Brotman
MANUFACTURING DIRECTOR   Gerald Levine
SYSTEMS MANAGER   Lindsey Ottman
PRODUCTION MANAGER   Joseph Romano
PRODUCTION COORDINATOR   Marie Claire Cebrián

The Encyclopedia of Health
SENIOR EDITOR   Brian Feinberg

Staff for MEDICAL DIAGNOSIS
ASSOCIATE EDITOR   LaVonne Carlson-Finnerty
COPY EDITOR   Christopher Duffy
EDITORIAL ASSISTANT   Tamar Levovitz
PICTURE RESEARCHER   Sandy Jones
DESIGNER   Robert Yaffe

First Printing
1   3   5   7   9   8   6   4   2

Library of Congress Cataloging-in-Publication Data

Nardo, Don
   Medical diagnosis/by Don Nardo; introduction by C. Everett Koop.
      p. cm.—(The Encyclopedia of health)
   Includes bibliographical references and index.
   Summary: An examination of the techniques and tools used by early healers and modern physicians to uncover the signs of disease.
   ISBN 0-7910-0067-2
         0-7910-0494-5 (pbk.)
   1. Diagnosis—Juvenile literature. [1. Diagnosis. 2. Medical care. 3. Medicine—History.] I. Title. II. Series.   91-34788
RC71.3.N37 1992   CIP
616.07'5—dc20   AC

CONTENTS

THE ENCYCLOPEDIA OF
H E A L T H

THE HEALTHY BODY

The Circulatory System
Dental Health
The Digestive System
The Endocrine System
Exercise
Genetics & Heredity
The Human Body: An Overview
Hygiene
The Immune System
Memory & Learning
The Musculoskeletal System
The Nervous System
Nutrition
The Reproductive System
The Respiratory System
The Senses
Sleep
Speech & Hearing
Sports Medicine
Vision
Vitamins & Minerals

THE LIFE CYCLE

Adolescence
Adulthood
Aging
Childhood
Death & Dying
The Family
Friendship & Love
Pregnancy & Birth

MEDICAL ISSUES

Careers in Health Care
Environmental Health
Folk Medicine
Health Care Delivery
Holistic Medicine
Medical Ethics
Medical Fakes & Frauds
Medical Technology
Medicine & the Law
Occupational Health
Public Health

PSYCHOLOGICAL DISORDERS AND THEIR TREATMENT

Anxiety & Phobias
Child Abuse
Compulsive Behavior
Delinquency & Criminal Behavior
Depression
Diagnosing & Treating Mental Illness
Eating Habits & Disorders
Learning Disabilities
Mental Retardation
Personality Disorders
Schizophrenia
Stress Management
Suicide

MEDICAL DISORDERS AND THEIR TREATMENT

AIDS
Allergies
Alzheimer's Disease
Arthritis
Birth Defects
Cancer
The Common Cold
Diabetes
Emergency Medicine
Gynecological Disorders
Headaches
The Hospital
Kidney Disorders
Medical Diagnosis
The Mind-Body Connection
Mononucleosis and Other Infectious Diseases
Nuclear Medicine
Organ Transplants
Pain
Physical Handicaps
Poisons & Toxins
Prescription & OTC Drugs
Sexually Transmitted Diseases
Skin Disorders
Stroke & Heart Disease
Substance Abuse
Tropical Medicine

PREVENTION AND EDUCATION: THE KEYS TO GOOD HEALTH

C. Everett Koop, M.D., Sc.D.
former Surgeon General,
U.S. Public Health Service

The issue of health education has received particular attention in recent years because of the presence of AIDS in the news. But our response to this particular tragedy points up a number of broader issues that doctors, public health officials, educators, and the public face. In particular, it points up the necessity for sound health education for citizens of all ages.

Over the past 25 years this country has been able to bring about dramatic declines in the death rates for heart disease, stroke, accidents, and for people under the age of 45, cancer. Today, Americans generally eat better and take better care of themselves than ever before. Thus, with the help of modern science and technology, they have a better chance of surviving serious—even catastrophic—illnesses. That's the good news.

But, like every phonograph record, there's a flip side, and one with special significance for young adults. According to a report issued in 1979 by Dr. Julius Richmond, my predecessor as Surgeon General, Americans aged 15 to 24 had a higher death rate in 1979 than they did 20 years earlier. The causes: violent death and injury, alcohol and drug abuse, unwanted pregnancies, and sexually transmitted diseases. Adolescents are particularly vulnerable because they are beginning to explore their own sexuality and perhaps to experiment with drugs. The need for educating young people is critical, and the price of neglect is high.

Yet even for the population as a whole, our health is still far from what it could be. Why? A 1974 Canadian government report attributed all death and disease to four broad elements: inadequacies in the health care system, behavioral factors or unhealthy life-styles, environmental hazards, and human biological factors.

To be sure, there are diseases that are still beyond the control of even our advanced medical knowledge and techniques. And despite yearnings that are as old as the human race itself, there is no "fountain of youth" to ward off aging and death. Still, there is a solution to many of the problems that undermine sound health. In a word, that solution is prevention. Prevention, which includes health promotion and education, saves lives, improves the quality of life, and in the long run, saves money.

In the United States, organized public health activities and preventive medicine have a long history. Important milestones in this country or foreign breakthroughs adopted in the United States include the improvement of sanitary procedures and the development of pasteurized milk in the late 19th century and the introduction in the mid-20th century of effective vaccines against polio, measles, German measles, mumps, and other once-rampant diseases. Internationally, organized public health efforts began on a wide-scale basis with the International Sanitary Conference of 1851, to which 12 nations sent representatives. The World Health Organization, founded in 1948, continues these efforts under the aegis of the United Nations, with particular emphasis on combating communicable diseases and the training of health care workers.

Despite these accomplishments, much remains to be done in the field of prevention. For too long, we have had a medical care system that is science- and technology-based, focused, essentially, on illness and mortality. It is now patently obvious that both the social and the economic costs of such a system are becoming insupportable.

Implementing prevention—and its corollaries, health education and promotion—is the job of several groups of people.

First, the medical and scientific professions need to continue basic scientific research, and here we are making considerable progress. But increased concern with prevention will also have a decided impact on how primary care doctors practice medicine. With a shift to health-based rather than morbidity-based medicine, the role of the "new physician" will include a healthy dose of patient education.

Second, practitioners of the social and behavioral sciences—psychologists, economists, city planners—along with lawyers, business leaders, and government officials—must solve the practical and ethical dilemmas confronting us: poverty, crime, civil rights, literacy, education, employment, housing, sanitation, environmental protection, health care delivery systems, and so forth. All of these issues affect public health.

Third is the public at large. We'll consider that very important group in a moment.

Fourth, and the linchpin in this effort, is the public health profession—doctors, epidemiologists, teachers—who must harness the professional expertise of the first two groups and the common sense and cooperation of the third, the public. They must define the problems statistically and qualitatively and then help us set priorities for finding the solutions.

To a very large extent, improving those statistics is the responsibility of every individual. So let's consider more specifically what the role of the individual should be and why health education is so important to that role. First, and most obvious, individuals can protect themselves from illness and injury and thus minimize their need for professional medical care. They can eat nutritious food; get adequate exercise; avoid tobacco, alcohol, and drugs; and take prudent steps to avoid accidents. The proverbial "apple a day keeps the doctor away" is not so far from the truth, after all.

Second, individuals should actively participate in their own medical care. They should schedule regular medical and dental checkups. Should they develop an illness or injury, they should know when to treat themselves and when to seek professional help. To gain the maximum benefit from any medical treatment that they do require, individuals must become partners in that treatment. For instance, they should understand the effects and side effects of medications. I counsel young physicians that there is no such thing as too much information when talking with patients. But the corollary is the patient must know enough about the nuts and bolts of the healing process to understand what the doctor is telling him or her. That is at least partially the patient's responsibility.

Education is equally necessary for us to understand the ethical and public policy issues in health care today. Sometimes individuals will encounter these issues in making decisions about their own treatment or that of family members. Other citizens may encounter them as jurors in medical malpractice cases. But we all become involved, indirectly, when we elect our public officials, from school board members to the president. Should surrogate parenting be legal? To what extent is drug testing desirable, legal, or necessary? Should there be public funding for family planning, hospitals, various types of medical research, and other medical care for the indigent? How should we allocate scant technological resources, such as kidney dialysis and organ transplants? What is the proper role of government in protecting the rights of patients?

What are the broad goals of public health in the United States today? In 1980, the Public Health Service issued a report aptly entitled *Promoting Health—Preventing Disease: Objectives for the Nation*. This report expressed its goals in terms of mortality and in terms of intermediate goals in education and health improvement. It identified 15 major concerns: controlling high blood pressure; improving family planning; improving pregnancy care and infant health; increasing the rate of immunization; controlling sexually transmitted diseases; controlling the presence of toxic agents and radiation in the environment; improving occupational safety and health; preventing accidents; promoting water fluoridation and dental health; controlling infectious diseases; decreasing smoking; decreasing alcohol and drug abuse; improving nutrition; promoting physical fitness and exercise; and controlling stress and violent behavior.

For healthy adolescents and young adults (ages 15 to 24), the specific goal was a 20% reduction in deaths, with a special focus on motor vehicle injuries and alcohol and drug abuse. For adults (ages 25 to 64), the aim was 25% fewer deaths, with a concentration on heart attacks, strokes, and cancers.

Smoking is perhaps the best example of how individual behavior can have a direct impact on health. Today, cigarette smoking is recognized as the single most important preventable cause of death in our society. It is responsible for more cancers and more cancer deaths than any other known agent; is a prime risk factor for heart and blood vessel disease, chronic bronchitis, and emphysema; and is a frequent cause of complications in pregnancies and of babies born prematurely, underweight, or with potentially fatal respiratory and cardiovascular problems.

Since the release of the Surgeon General's first report on smoking in 1964, the proportion of adult smokers has declined substantially, from 43% in 1965 to 30.5% in 1985. Since 1965, 37 million people have quit smoking. Although there is still much work to be done if we are to become a "smoke-free society," it is heartening to note that public health and public education efforts—such as warnings on cigarette packages and bans on broadcast advertising—have already had significant effects.

In 1835, Alexis de Tocqueville, a French visitor to America, wrote, "In America the passion for physical well-being is general." Today, as then, health and fitness are front-page items. But with the greater scientific and technological resources now available to us, we are in a far stronger position to make good health care available to everyone. And with the greater technological threats to us as we approach the 21st century, the need to do so is more urgent than ever before. Comprehensive information about basic biology, preventive medicine, medical and surgical treatments, and related ethical and public policy issues can help you arm yourself with the knowledge you need to be healthy throughout your life.

FOREWORD

Dale C. Garell, M.D.

Advances in our understanding of health and disease during the 20th century have been truly remarkable. Indeed, it could be argued that modern health care is one of the greatest accomplishments in all of human history. In the early 20th century, improvements in sanitation, water treatment, and sewage disposal reduced death rates and increased longevity. Previously untreatable illnesses can now be managed with antibiotics, immunizations, and modern surgical techniques. Discoveries in the fields of immunology, genetic diagnosis, and organ transplantation are revolutionizing the prevention and treatment of disease. Modern medicine is even making inroads against cancer and heart disease, two of the leading causes of death in the United States.

Although there is much to be proud of, medicine continues to face enormous challenges. Science has vanquished diseases such as smallpox and polio, but new killers, most notably AIDS, confront us. Moreover, we now victimize ourselves with what some have called "diseases of choice," or those brought on by drug and alcohol abuse, bad eating habits, and mismanagement of the stresses and strains of contemporary life. The very technology that is doing so much to prolong life has brought with it previously unimaginable ethical dilemmas related to issues of death and dying. The rising cost of health care is a matter of central concern to us all. And violence in the form of automobile accidents, homicide, and suicide remains the major killer of young adults.

In the past, most people were content to leave health care and medical treatment in the hands of professionals. But since the 1960s, the consumer of medical care—that is, the patient—has assumed an increasingly central role in the management of his or her own health. There has also been a new emphasis placed on prevention: People are recognizing that their own actions can help prevent many of the conditions that have caused death and disease in the past. This accounts for the growing commitment to good nutrition and regular exercise, for the increasing number of people who are choosing not to smoke, and for a new moderation in people's drinking habits.

People want to know more about themselves and their own health. They are curious about their body: its anatomy, physiology, and biochemistry. They want to keep up with rapidly evolving medical technologies and procedures. They are willing to educate themselves about common disorders and diseases so that they can be full partners in their own health care.

THE ENCYCLOPEDIA OF HEALTH is designed to provide the basic knowledge that readers will need if they are to take significant responsibility for their own health. It is also meant to serve as a frame of reference for further study and exploration. The encyclopedia is divided into five subsections: The Healthy Body; The Life Cycle; Medical Disorders & Their Treatment; Psychological Disorders & Their Treatment; and Medical Issues. For each topic covered by the encyclopedia, we present the essential facts about the relevant biology; the symptoms, diagnosis, and treatment of common diseases and disorders; and ways in which you can prevent or reduce the severity of health problems when that is possible. The encyclopedia also projects what may lie ahead in the way of future treatment or prevention strategies.

The broad range of topics and issues covered in the encyclopedia reflects that human health encompasses physical, psychological, social, environmental, and spiritual well-being. Just as the mind and the body are inextricably linked, so, too, is the individual an integral part of the wider world that comprises his or her family, society, and environment. To discuss health in its broadest aspect it is necessary to explore the many ways in which it is connected to such fields as law, social science, public policy, economics, and even religion. And so, the encyclopedia is meant to be a bridge between science, medical technology, the world at large, and you. I hope that it will inspire you to pursue in greater depth particular areas of interest and that you will take advantage of the suggestions for further reading and the lists of resources and organizations that can provide additional information.

CHAPTER 1

THE HISTORY OF DIAGNOSIS

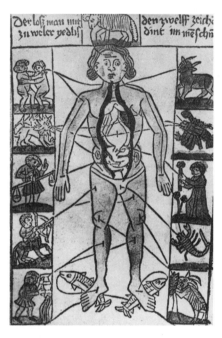

Diagnosis has been called "the art of distinguishing one disease from another." However, early healers often attributed physical ailments to spiritual conditions, as depicted in this 1475 calendar.

The term *diagnosis* comes from the two Greek words, *gnosis*, meaning "to know" and *dia*, meaning "more." Thus, a diagnosis helps the doctor to know more; to distinguish or discern the signals of illness.

In the 17th and 18th centuries, doctors used the term *diagnostics* to refer to the distinguishing *signs* and *symptoms* of a particular disease or condition. Symptoms are the problems a patient experiences and reports to a doctor, whereas signs are problems that the doctor observes independently. Today, doctors think of diagnosis not as the symptoms themselves but as the process of identifying symptoms by careful investigation. Medical authorities often refer to diagnosis as the art of distinguishing one disease from another.

As modern medical techniques became more complex and diagnostic tools grew correspondingly advanced, doctors began to classify diagnosis in many different ways. For example, diagnosis based strictly on physical examinination of the patient is referred to as *physical* or *anatomical diagnosis*, and diagnosis based on tests done by lab machines is called *laboratory diagnosis*. In certain cases a patient's primary physician will recommend that he or she visit a specialist concerning a special problem. Often this consultant is better informed about the specific techniques required to diagnose the patient's condition.

Many types of diagnostic procedures are available. In *bacteriological diagnosis*, a doctor identifies an illness by studying the bacteria in the patient's blood, urine, or other substances. Other techniques include *X-ray diagnosis* and *electrocardiographic diagnosis*. No matter what the diagnostic procedure is called, the goal is always the same: to observe and analyze the symptoms and signs in order to identify the illness.

In addition to revealing a specific illness, a correct diagnosis allows the doctor to make a *prognosis*. A prognosis is a prediction of

Primitive medical practitioners in eastern Europe and northern Asia were called shamans. These healers and their traditions still exist today.

how long the illness will last or how quickly a specific treatment will take effect. Thus, accurate diagnosis is necessary for effective prognosis and recovery.

ILLNESS IN ANCIENT DAYS

Disease and illness are not new phenomena; they have continually plagued human beings and their more primitive mammalian ancestors. Scientists who study ancient peoples and societies often find clues to past medical problems when they examine skeletons, teeth, and other remains of long-dead humans.

Some of the earliest examples of human illness are found in Neanderthals, the people who inhabited caves in Europe, northern Africa, and western Asia between 100,000 and 30,000 years ago. Experts who have studied the fossilized teeth of Neanderthals have discovered that these early humans suffered from tooth decay and gum diseases just as modern people do. An examination of their bones reveals that the Neanderthals also suffered from *arthritis* (inflammation of the joints), curvature of the spine, and other skeletal problems.

When modern medical experts first examined the remains of ancient Egyptian mummies, they found evidence of a host of diseases and medical conditions that still affect people today. Scientists have identified such problems as hardening of the arteries, pneumonia, urinary infections, gallstones, and parasites in the mummies.

Native American healers were referred to as medicine men because they knew which plants might cure an ailment and where to find them. This 1850 engraving shows a medicine man shaking a gourd rattle to invoke the gods after treating a patient with medicine.

15

The Early Healers

Like people today, ancient humans sought ways to fight disease and heal themselves. They often put their trust in local experts—people who had accumulated a great deal of knowledge about sickness and the methods to treat and prevent it. Today, healers are called doctors, but through the centuries people used different terms to describe them. Inhabitants of northern Asia and eastern Europe called them *shamans*, whereas natives of central Africa used the name *diviners* or *witch doctors*. The North American Indians referred to healers as *medicine men* because they found and administered the medicines that stopped or minimized pain and suffering.

Like modern doctors, early healers had to diagnose illnesses before they could treat them. Today's physicians use diagnostic methods that reflect their knowledge of disease and illness. For example, they know that a buildup of cholesterol in the blood can coat the insides of the arteries and restrict blood flow. If a patient shows signs of a restricted flow, a doctor automatically performs tests to measure the patient's cholesterol levels. In the same way, premodern healers used diagnostic methods based on the prevailing views of what made people sick. Generally speaking, these early ideas about the causes of disease and illness were quite different from those accepted by modern doctors.

Premodern Views of Sickness

Although primitive concepts about sickness varied from one society to the next, most fell into a few broad categories. One common belief was that illness was caused by *sorcery*, or black magic. People with magical powers could supposedly summon supernatural forces to strike out at their victims by causing them to become ill.

A sorcerer or sorceress was thought to have employed one of two methods to produce illness. First, he or she might have constructed a small doll or other image of the victim and then stabbed or pounded the image. The pain, it was believed, would be transferred directly to the victim. This method survived into the 20th century as part of the religion known as *Voodoo*, which is still practiced in some Caribbean islands. A sorcerer might also have tried to cause illness by saying a

Historically, people have believed that healers have a privileged line of communication with the gods. This engraving depicts a healer asking divine forgiveness for a patient believed to have been made ill by a god.

magic spell over a discarded piece of the victim's nail clippings, hair, or excrement.

Another concept of sickness had to do with the breaking of a *taboo*. A taboo was a social or religious rule, supposedly established by the gods, by which people were expected to abide. Those who broke the taboo were believed to have incurred the wrath of the gods, and punishment often took the form of disease or physical deformity.

Another widespread belief was that demons or evil spirits invaded people's bodies, bringing disease and pain. For example, the ancient Mesopotamians believed that a specific demon was responsible for each separate symptom. Fever was caused by the demonic spirit Nergal, and Tiu inflicted people with headaches. The worst of these demons were the Evil Seven, who caused serious ailments without warning. Fearing their wrath, Mesopotamian doctors refrained from treating patients on the seventh, 14th, or 21st day of sickness—or on any date divisible by 7.

Another premodern belief was that disease resulted from a person's loss of soul. A demon, ghost, sorcerer, or mischievous god was thought to steal the soul, causing serious illness. To cure the patient, the healer endeavored to return the soul to the body. How a healer was able to diagnose a loss of soul remains unclear, but that the effort was made underscores the influence of supernatural beliefs on early medical practices.

Egyptian doctors were among the first to examine the patient's body and link symptoms to specific problems, enabling them to offer appropriate treatment. In this illustration, an Egyptian doctor is treating a shoulder wound.

EARLY ATTEMPTS AT DIAGNOSIS

Ancient healers began diagnosis by analyzing the nature of the illness. Among the most primitive, preliterate peoples, the healer first questioned the victim to find out whether he or she had committed an offense or broken a taboo. The diagnosis sometimes continued with the healer going into a trance and consulting the gods. Treatment might then consist of the patient begging forgiveness of the god who was slighted.

Premodern healers also diagnosed illness by *divination*, the reading of signs in various objects and animals. For example, a healer might throw a handful of bones in the dirt and make a diagnosis based on the pattern they formed. Another method involved poisoning an animal and watching its reactions as it died. Different reactions indicated different causes for a human illness.

In some cases, when a healer believed that the patient had broken a taboo or been inhabited by a demon, the patient was subjected to ordeals of fire or water. The healer believed that burning or submersing the patient would force an admission of guilt in order to reveal the problem. Unfortunately, the patient, rather than recovering, often died during diagnosis.

Logical Approaches

In general, a culture's healers began to lose fewer patients to death when its medical practices became more scientific and safe. The ancient Egyptians observed that no matter which factors caused an illness, the symptoms were always expressed in physical form. Therefore, to diagnose the problem, a physical examination of the patient was required. Egyptian doctors used their fingers to probe various parts of the body. They also felt the patient's pulse, looked at the eyes, and examined the urine and feces.

Egyptian doctors usually assumed that each symptom resulted from a separate disease or ailment. For example, fever, skin rash, and swelling were diagnosed as distinct medical problems and often treated individually. By contrast, modern doctors recognize that these problems might all be symptoms of a single disease.

In ancient India as well, doctors used extensive physical examinations for diagnosis. The patient was questioned to determine certain facts about the illness, such as how long he or she had been suffering, where the pain was located, and how severe it was. The healer might have also asked whether the person had recently lost a lot of weight—a clue that helped analyze the ailment. Indian doctors also took the patient's pulse and classified dozens of pulse rates.

Indian doctors were among the first to recognize the importance of observing a patient's pulse. They classified dozens of pulse rates and also learned to detect diabetes by testing urine for a sweet taste.

As in Egypt, the physical exam included a study of the feces and urine, and Indian doctors learned to administer urine taste tests. They recognized that people with *diabetes*, an abnormal condition characterized by excessive excretion of urine, have urine that tastes sweet, a discovery Europeans did not make until centuries later.

Intrigued by Classification

Early Chinese doctors used many of the same diagnostic techniques as their Indian counterparts. Chinese healers questioned the patient, then proceeded with physical observations, concentrating primarily on the pulse and the tongue. The Chinese were fascinated with variations among pulse rates. At least 51 basic types of pulse were recognized. In the *Muo-Ching*, an important Chinese medical treatise, 10 volumes were devoted to medical diagnosis achieved by reading the pulse.

Similarly, Chinese physicians counted at least 37 different shades of the tongue, each of which might have been a sign of a specific illness. Even after a major disease was recognized, the diagnosis was not over, because the illness might take many different forms. For instance, 42 separate forms of smallpox could be described. These elaborate classifications may have made it difficult for Chinese doctors to diagnose a problem and choose a specific treatment.

Although the Middle Ages brought few advances in the scientific approach to diagnosis, European physicians continued to use techniques developed earlier. This 1555 woodcut portrays a doctor continuing the tradition of feeling a patient's pulse.

Early Greek doctors also recognized many different versions of each ailment, primarily because the Greeks, like the Egyptians, saw specific symptoms as separate ailments. For example, they described varying appearances of blood spit up by patients as separate problems. Similarly, the Greeks also believed there were 7 bile diseases and 12 bladder diseases.

Although Greek doctors recognized many medical ailments, they spent little time on diagnosis. A physician might touch, smell, or occasionally shake the victim and listen for movement of excess internal fluids. The doctor might also observe the person's temperature and pulse. But most Greek doctors felt that an elaborate diagnosis was unnecessary, and they were much more interested in prognosis and treatment. They emphasized the overall health of the patient and tended to treat the whole body rather than the individual parts. Part of the philosophy of Greek healing was the belief that nature was the strongest single force in the healing process and that doctors should act only to assist the natural effects.

MEDIEVAL DIAGNOSIS

For about a thousand years, during the period known as the Middle Ages or Dark Ages, medical practices barely progressed, and in Europe, often regressed. Doctors relied on diagnostic techniques handed down from past healers, especially the Greeks. Physicians tended to lump symptoms together into broad categories, such as *epidemic* (spreading rapidly through a community) or *endemic* (localized in a single geographic area with a controlled risk of spreading). Treatment for a wide range of symptoms often consisted of *bleeding* (drawing blood from an arm or leg), based on the belief that illness was due to impurities or evil substances in the blood.

Techniques used by the Arabs of North Africa and the Middle East were an exception to the backwardness of medieval medical practices. Although Arab doctors often consulted the stars and other supernatural sources in their diagnosis, some of their methods resembled modern medical practices. They took their patients' past behavior into account and checked their eyes, ears, and any unusual swellings on the body.

Certain historic medical techniques may have done more harm than good. The dubious practice of bleeding—causing a patient to bleed in order to release evil spirits or impurities—is shown in this James Gillray (1757–1815) caricature.

They also took the patients' pulse and examined the feces, urine, saliva, and other bodily substances.

In fact, Arab physicians became extremely adept at diagnosing illness by studying urine. They considered such factors as the urine's color, taste, smell, and the amount of sediments it contained. Their expertise in this area became so renowned that a half-filled urine flask became the recognized sign of Arab doctors.

But even the Arabs could accomplish only limited results without more advanced diagnostic tools. There were no *stethoscopes*, thermometers, or tools for chemical analyses available at the time. And doctors still believed in supernatural and religious explanations for sickness—beliefs that made accurate diagnosis difficult and sometimes impossible. For better diagnosis, humanity had to wait for the introduction of modern medical concepts and tools in the 18th and 19th centuries.

CHAPTER 2

THE DEVELOPMENT OF MODERN DIAGNOSIS

The Italian physician Santorio Santorio (1561–1636) proposed that the body operates like a machine, and therefore its problems could be detected by its changes.

Medical treatment in ancient times was often primitive and inadequate for two reasons. First, healers did not possess suitable tools to diagnose illness properly. Second, people, including doctors, were ignorant about the causes of disease. Because an accurate diagnosis was often lacking, effective treatment was rare. The invention of modern diagnostic instruments and the acquisition of knowledge about what actually causes disease were keys that helped unlock the door to modern medical treatment. These advances occurred over a span of nearly 300 years, beginning in the 17th century.

EARLY INSTRUMENTS OF PRECISION

Santorio Santorio, a professor at Italy's University of Padua, introduced some of the first precise diagnostic instruments between 1600 and 1625. His belief that the body worked like a machine, in a mechanical way, led him to develop several devices for measuring its changes.

His initial contribution was an accurate method of taking the pulse. It seems that Santorio's friend, the renowned scientist Galileo, watched a lamp swinging in the cathedral at Pisa and timed the swings by feeling his pulse. Santorio hit upon the idea of reversing Galileo's procedure. He attached a weight to a cord and swung it back and forth, then trimmed the cord to various lengths in order to make the swings match the rates of different people's pulses. Santorio then used the various cord lengths to mark measurements on a scale that could then be used to determine anyone's pulse rate.

Santorio also used a crude thermometer that Galileo had devised to record the patients' temperatures in various states of illness. He

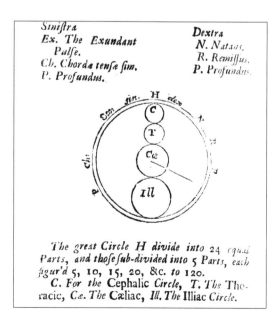

In 1707, the English physician Sir John Floyer (1649–1734) invented the first device to accurately measure the pulse. This woodcut diagrams the instrument, called a pulse watch.

thus acquired a rudimentary understanding of how extremes in body temperature reflect the degree of sickness. In addition, he studied the phenomenon of weight loss during illness by accurately weighing both healthy and ill patients on a regular basis. This practice allowed him to measure how much water weight people lost during illness as well as during exercise or other activities.

Most doctors in Santorio's time did not recognize the importance of his work, and acceptance of these techniques progressed slowly. It was not until 1707 that doctors began to use accurate timing of the pulse as a standard procedure. In that year, an English physician, Sir John Floyer, published *The Physician's Pulse Watch*, in which he described a pulse-timing instrument of his own invention. The device ran for 60 seconds, during which Floyer counted the number of pulse beats.

PERCUSSION

The 18th century's most important diagnostic development was the discovery of *percussion* by Leopold Auenbrugger von Auenbrugg. Percussion is the technique of tapping the body in specific places to produce sounds that give information about the internal organs. The human body is full of air-filled spaces, such as the insides of the lungs and stomach, and when these areas are tapped, a hollow, resonant sound is produced. By contrast, when the lungs are filled with fluid, as they are in the case of pneumonia or infection, percussion produces a dull sound.

This lithograph portrays Leopold Auenbrugger von Auenbrugg (1722–1809), who first developed percussion, the diagnostic technique of listening to the body while tapping it as a way to assess internal conditions.

Auenbrugger was the son of an Austrian innkeeper and often watched his father tapping wine casks. The different sounds produced indicated how much wine was left in the containers.

Auenbrugger reasoned that he could use the same technique to aid in medical diagnosis, and he began experimenting on dead human bodies. He worked for seven years, injecting varying amounts of water into the lungs and other body parts and then practicing percussion. Auenbrugger, an accomplished musician, trained to hear small differences in tone and pitch, was skilled in interpreting the many sounds his tapping produced.

In 1761, Auenbrugger published the results of his work in a short book, *Inventum Novum* (New Invention). Unfortunately, the medical community showed little interest in percussion, and few doctors, even in Auenbrugger's native Austria, tried the technique. Nearly 40 years later, a young French doctor, Jean-Nicolas Corvisart des Marets, arrived in Austria and revived interest in Auenbrugger's work. Corvisart expanded *Inventum Novum* from 95 to 440 pages and gave full credit to Auenbrugger as the discoverer of percussion. Combining the technique with his own knowledge, from performing autopsies, Corvisart helped found the most advanced center for medical diagnosis of its time, the Paris Clinical School.

AMPLIFYING SOUNDS FROM THE BODY

Although percussion opened up new vistas in medical diagnosis, most doctors still had difficulty distinguishing among the many similar sounds they heard when pressing their ears up against the chest or abdomen. One of Corvisart's former pupils at the Paris Clinical School, a French physician named René Laënnec, was determined to find a better way to hear sounds produced by the human body.

One day while on his way to visit a patient, Laënnec observed some children playing in a park. One child tapped a pin on a long beam of wood, while the other children put their ears to the other end of the beam and listened. Seeing the children transmitting messages in this way, he recognized the potential of sound transmission for physical diagnosis. Reaching his patient's house, he rolled up a pad of paper and

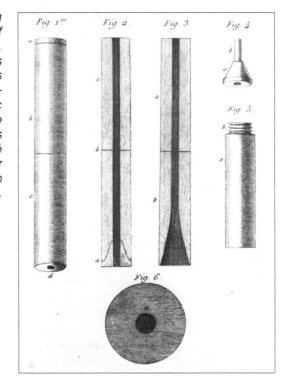

This 1819 engraving shows the design of the first stethoscope. By amplifying sounds inside the body, this instrument greatly advanced the diagnostic use of percussion. The stethoscope was invented by René Laënnec, who later became Napoléon Bonaparte's physician.

placed it against the patient's chest. Laënnec was elated to find that he could hear the sounds of the heart and other body parts much more clearly than before.

Laënnec soon constructed better versions of his hollow paper tube. He named his new instrument the stethoscope, combining the Greek words for *chest* and *explore*. For three years, he performed exhaustive tests with the device on both patients and dead human bodies, carefully detailing his observations. As he developed the instrument, he also originated a methodical approach to diagnosis referred to as the *anatomical-clinical method*. In 1819, Laënnec published the results of his work. One of its first important contributions included a successful means of diagnosing *tuberculosis* (TB), a contagious disease of the lungs. Before the invention of the stethoscope, doctors found it difficult, if not impossible, to distinguish between TB and many other conditions characterized by fluid in the lungs.

Acceptance of the stethoscope as a medical tool was slow at first because the principle of percussion itself was still unknown in many parts of the world. But within 10 years, doctors as far away as the United States were using the device. In time, the stethoscope became a universal symbol of physicians. The instrument, in a sense, placed the doctor's ear inside the body, making it possible to diagnose hundreds of conditions accurately. As one medical historian says, "Laënnec . . . did more than provide the medical profession with a somewhat more dignified symbol than the medieval urinal; he opened up a whole new world for medicine."

DISCOVERING THE CAUSE OF DISEASE

The field of medical diagnosis was greatly enhanced by the discovery that *germs*, microorganisms invisible to the unaided eye, cause many diseases. Scientists had known of the existence of germs for nearly 200 years but had not suspected that these microscopic creatures had any link to illness. Before the mid-19th century, doctors, like everyone else, assumed that diseases had magical or divine origins. Because of this orientation, physicians routinely misinterpreted symptoms of various conditions or failed to recognize important clues that might have helped them identify and treat diseases.

In 1854, the French chemist Louis Pasteur discovered that microorganisms caused food spoilage and the fermentation of wine from grape juice. Pasteur reasoned that, if germs damaged food and drink, they

In 1854, Louis Pasteur (1822–95) made the famous discovery that microscopic organisms, or germs, were linked to food spoilage. This 1899 engraving depicts the French chemist in his laboratory.

In 1874, the German scientist Robert Koch (1843–1910) provided proof that human disease is also caused by germs.

might also harm living tissue. He and other researchers set out to prove the connection between germs and disease. In 1876, German scientist Robert Koch provided the crucial evidence when he isolated the *bacteria* (members of the class of microscopic plants that often spread disease in humans) that cause *anthrax*, a disease common to cattle and other domesticated animals. In 1882, Koch also isolated the bacteria that cause TB, firmly establishing that microorganisms are dangerous to human beings.

The medical community's acceptance of the germ theory stimulated new approaches to the art of diagnosis. For example, doctors began to draw blood from patients and examine it under *microscopes* (instruments that use lenses to make an enlarged image of a minute object) in order to detect these microorganisms. The presence of certain germs in the blood either confirmed or disproved the initial diagnosis made in the doctor's physical examination. Many other laboratory and chemical tests were devised that expanded the abilities of medical personnel to diagnose illness.

The Man Who Discovered X Rays

Physicist Wilhelm Conrad Röntgen, the first scientist to recognize the existence of X rays, was born in Lennep, Germany, in 1845. After receiving a Ph.D. from the University of Zurich, in Switzerland, in 1869, he held several teaching positions prior to becoming director of the Physical Institute at the University of Würzburg, Germany, in 1885.

It was here that Röntgen experimented with *cathode rays*, that is, streams of negatively charged subatomic particles called *electrons* given off by a *cathode* in a *vacuum tube* (a tube from which the air has been removed).

During one experiment, he noticed that a *fluorescent screen* (a screen coated with a material that gives off light when exposed to certain types of radiation) positioned some distance away from the vacuum tube began to glow. This occurred even though the vacuum tube had been covered by thick paper that prevented ordinary light from passing through. Röntgen correctly theorized that along with cathode rays, other, unknown rays capable of penetrating the paper were being generated by the tube and were striking the screen.

Subsequent experiments revealed that the mysterious rays passed though many materials that blocked ordinary light. Röntgen noticed that the rays also affected photographic plates, an observation that suggested an intriguing possibility: that the plates could be placed behind a human body and the rays passed through the body to record internal images.

Some of Röntgen's colleagues called the newfound rays *Roentgen rays*, but the scientist himself preferred to call them X rays.

Although Röntgen's work earned him the first Nobel Prize for physics (1901), he did not wish to exploit his X-ray research for financial gain and therefore did not patent his results. According to the biography *The Life of Wilhelm Conrad Röntgen, Discoverer of the X Ray*, by W. Robert Nitske, the physicist stated that all of his information on X rays should be made available to the scientific community. In that way, he hoped, other re-

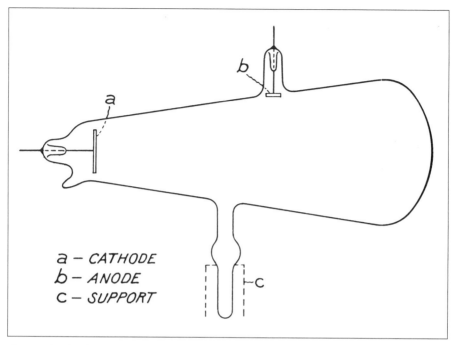

a – CATHODE
b – ANODE
c – SUPPORT

An early device used to generate X rays.

searchers would be free to develop X-ray technology and achieve the greatest public benefit. Nitske's book quotes Röntgen as insisting, "[A]ccording to the good tradition of the German university professor, I am of the opinion that their discoveries and inventions belong to humanity and that they should not in any way be hampered by patents, licenses, contracts, or be controlled by any one group."

For a time, however, X rays were used not only for serious research but also for public entertainment. According to the Nitske book, for example, in the late 1890s, Columbia University's H. D. Hawks gave X-ray demonstrations at Bloomingdale's department store in New York. For a period of several weeks, working for two to three hours per day, he took X rays of his own body. Unfortunately, the harmful effects of heavy exposure to X rays were not yet well known. Hawks suffered hair loss, skin damage similar to a severe sunburn, and impaired vision.

Röntgen died in 1923. In addition to his work with X rays, he also made important contributions to the studies of elasticity, gases, and polarized light.

MORE ADVANCED DIAGNOSTIC TOOLS

After the confirmation of the germ theory of disease, many doctors and scientists turned their attention to further improving diagnostic instruments and methods. In the 1880s, England's Sir James Mackenzie invented a device that took pulse rates from the wrist and neck simultaneously. This procedure helped him measure differences and pinpoint where irregularities in the pulse occurred. Since pulse rates indicate the heart's pumping action and blood flow, Mackenzie's instrument made significant contributions to understanding heart conditions and circulatory problems.

X Rays

One of the most important medical milestones was the discovery of X rays in 1895 by the German physicist Wilhelm Conrad Röntgen. He found that passing X rays through the body and recording them on a plate of chemically sensitive material produces images of the inside of

Wilhelm Conrad Röntgen (1845–1923) was the German physicist who discovered X rays in 1895. In 1901, he was awarded a Nobel Prize for his various achievements in the field of physics.

the body. Doctors could now examine X-ray images to observe internal irregularities, such as defects or breaks in the bones, and make more reliable diagnoses. This technique created an immediate sensation in medical circles, and hospitals around the world hurried to acquire X-ray equipment.

X-ray technology received a further boost in 1898, when Walter B. Cannon discovered the process of *fluoroscopy*. In his first experiments, Cannon fed lab animals mixtures of barium and other substances opaque to X rays. Because the X rays did not penetrate the barium mixtures, these solutions showed up plainly on fluorescent X-ray screens placed behind the subjects. Researchers followed the course of the mixtures as they flowed through the esophagus, into the stomach, and then into the intestines. Within months, fluoroscopy was used on human subjects to check the flow of substances through the body.

The discovery of X-ray technology was a giant step forward in the field of medical diagnosis. Many internal problems, previously invisible to doctors, could now be detected and studied. For instance, TB, one of the world's most dreaded diseases, could be identified and treated early in its progress. Some cancers could be seen when they

This photograph of Walter B. Cannon (1871–1945) was made in 1908, 10 years afer his discovery of fluoroscopy. In this technique, a patient swallows a substance that X rays cannot penetrate enabling doctors to trace the substance's path through the body.

were still small enough to remove surgically. In addition, doctors could observe heart size, heart defects, fluid in the lungs, enlargements of the kidneys and spleen, and many other internal phenomena.

Sphygmomanometer

At the same time that the X-ray process was emerging, important advances were being made in measuring blood pressure. In 1896, Italian researcher Scipione Riva-Rocci invented the modern method for taking blood pressure, using a rubber bag pumped up to restrict the flow of blood temporarily in the arm. This restriction decreases the pulse at the wrist, so the doctor can hear the blood flow better at the bend of the elbow, where the pulse coincides with the contraction of the heart. Using Riva-Rocci's invention, the *sphygmomanometer*, doctors can detect irregularities in blood flow and heartbeat and use this data for diagnosis.

In the 20th century, many other diagnostic tools and methods have been invented. Specific tests included the *basal metabolism test*, which shows the amount of oxygen a person consumes at rest, and *skin scratch tests*, which reveal the presence of TB and other diseases. Modern diagnostic devices include the *ophthalmoscope*, used to inspect the retina in the eye, and the *gastroscope*, used to view the interior of the stomach. In addition, medical experts now infuse dyes opaque to X rays to inspect the kidneys, liver, and other organs, and complex equipment has been invented for detailed examination of the bodily fluids and organs such as the heart, lungs, and brain. Many of these modern devices and procedures will be explored in later chapters.

CHAPTER 3

MODERN DIAGNOSIS: THE EXAMINATION

Doctors often try to put a patient at ease when conducting a physical examination. A patient who is comfortable is more likely to help the doctor gather enough medical information for an accurate diagnosis.

Medical diagnosis is accomplished by two basic procedures: gathering information about the patient and the illness, then analyzing that information to establish the prognosis and treatment. The process of collecting information, usually referred to as the *examination*, generally involves recording data that the patient provides and physically scrutinizing the patient.

The examination process can be divided into four general steps. They include recording the patient's medical history, examining the patient physically, conducting tests using special techniques and lab machines, and observing how the illness progresses. Each of these methods provides the doctor with facts that offer important clues to the nature of the illness.

TAKING THE HISTORY

Recording the patient's medical history is important to diagnosis for a number of reasons. First, while the patient communicates his or her history, the doctor and patient establish a rapport that carries through to the treatment period. The doctor attempts to create a positive atmosphere, urges the patient to be as open and honest as possible, and tries to calm any fears the patient may have about his or her condition.

From the history, the doctor learns about diseases or conditions the patient has had earlier in life. These factors may indicate that the patient is more susceptible to certain physical problems than other people are or that one of these conditions is a recurring one. If the patient has suffered any unusual or serious injuries in the past, the doctor needs to know, because a prior injury could be contributing to the patient's present condition.

The patient is also questioned about illnesses suffered by his or her blood relatives. This information is important because genetic factors that affect several members of the patient's family may offer clues to the patient's problem. For instance, if the patient's parents or siblings have diabetes, the doctor will be especially alert to any signs of that condition during the physical examination. Conditions such as epilepsy, cancer, hypertension, and allergies also tend to be more prevalent in certain families.

The history also reveals other important information for forming a correct diagnosis. For example, the patient's workplace might have some bearing on the problem. If the patient works around chemicals or other dangerous materials, he or she may have been exposed to toxic fumes. Or perhaps the patient is affected by radiation, loud noises, unusual muscle or eye strains, or other factors in the work environment. The doctor records whether the patient has taken or still takes drugs of any kind, either for medical or recreational purposes. The patient also

A medical history informs the doctor of many aspects of a patient's life. For example, a physician should know if a patient works in potentially harmful surroundings, such as these engineers who are checking the Three Mile Island nuclear plant.

discusses drinking, smoking, sleeping, and eating habits, all of which could have a serious bearing on his or her health.

In taking the medical history, the doctor directly and indirectly asks for specific information about various parts and systems of the patient's body. For instance, the doctor or nurse may ask, "Have you recently suffered from unusual fatigue or episodes of chills? Have you noticed any unusual swelling or pain? Have you had any trouble or pain while urinating or noticed that your urine had an unusual color?" Other common questions involve the skin, eyes, ears, mouth and throat, breasts, breathing, stomach and appetite, and bones. Physicians also need to know any facts concerning the use of drugs.

Some of these questions take on special significance after the patient describes the history of the illness itself. The doctor asks the patient to recount as accurately as possible the specific symptoms of the illness, such as pain, shortness of breath, sore throat, nausea, vomiting, headaches, and bleeding. The physician also tries to determine the order in which the symptoms appeared, how long they have persisted, whether any have disappeared since the first occurrence, and whether this is the first time the patient has noticed these symptoms.

Before any physical examination takes place, the patient's history provides the doctor with valuable clues to the patient's condition. The doctor begins to piece together a picture of the problem, quickly eliminating the possibility of certain conditions while narrowing in on others.

The following modified excerpt from the book *Health Assessment,* by Lois Malasanos et al, presents a typical format for a health history when the patient is admitted to a hospital:

CLIENT: John Donald Doe

ADDRESS, TELEPHONE, BIRTHDATE

OCCUPATION: offset printer, but has been on disability for one year

CHIEF COMPLAINT: "Pain in the left side of stomach for two days."

PRESENT ILLNESS: This is the fifth hospital admission for this 29-year-old white, unemployed, separated male who has been drinking an average of 2 to 3 fifths of hard liquor daily. Total past admissions number eight. None of these [has] been for abdominal complaints. Also has a history of drug abuse and gastric ulcer. Chronological story:

- 14 years prior to admission (PTA) Began drinking heavily.

- 7 years PTA Diagnosed as having a gastric ulcer. Had X rays at the time. Has complained of slight to moderate gastric discomfort and food intolerance intermittently since then. Appetite has been good. Meal patterns are erratic.

- 1 day PTA Had not been drinking the night before. Awoke at 7:00 A.M. and took several alcoholic drinks.

After an hour experienced nausea and vomiting after an attempt to drink orange juice. At 10:00 A.M. walked to his mother's home. On arriving, experienced a sharp, continuous pain in his upper left abdominal area. At bedtime, took a sleeping pill but it did not help him sleep. Rose at 9:00 A.M. and came directly to hospital.

PAST HISTORY:

Injuries—

- Age 9 (1954)—Hit in eye by rock. States [he] has had a permanent decrease in vision in that eye.
- Age 15 or 16 (1960 or 1961)—Fractured right ankle while playing football. Cast applied. Apparently healed.

Hospitalizations—

- Age 20 (1965)—Pneumonia. Hospitalized for two weeks. No follow-up.
- Age 26 (1971)—Drug overdose. In hospital for one week. Discharged against medical advice.
- Age 28 (1973)—Drug overdose. In hospital for two weeks. Discharged on methadone maintenance.

Other major illnesses—

- Age 28 (1973)—TB. On medications for one year. Off medications for past three months.

Allergies—none known.

Habits—

- cigarettes—smokes one pack a day since age 12.
- hard drugs—all types, including heroin.
- alcohol—started to drink heavily at age 16. Drinking decreased during period of drug addiction.
- coffee—drinks six to seven cups a day.

FAMILY HISTORY:

- Maternal and paternal grandparents deceased. Ages at death and causes of death unknown. Denies family history of diabetes, blood disorders, gout, obesity, coronary heart disease, cancer, epilepsy, or allergic disorders. Mother—age 52, alive and well. Father— deceased, age 50, cause unknown. Brother—deceased, age 20, drug overdose.

REVIEW OF [PHYSICAL] SYSTEMS:

- general—chronically ill; usual weight about 176 lb. States he has felt a generalized fatigue for over one year, since onset of TB. Cannot exercise. Denies chills.

- skin—soles of feet dry and scaling for six months. Small cracks at corners of mouth for one month. Denies cold sores.

- chest and respiratory system—denies pain, wheezing, asthma, or bronchitis. States he had one episode of hemoptysis (coughing up blood), 1968, associated with his ulcer.

- other categories in review—eyes, ears, oral cavity, neck, breasts, back, heart, bladder, and kidneys.

From this history, the doctor learns that Mr. Doe has consumed large amounts of alcohol and drugs over the years. The patient has also suffered from TB and a stomach ulcer. The physician also notes that the patient smokes and recently has been drinking alcohol and eating erratically, all of which can irritate an ulcer. The doctor suspects that Mr. Doe's ulcer has worsened and will look for clues to support that hypothesis during the physical examination.

Knowing that Mr. Doe suffered from an ulcer, the doctor would also be particularly interested in the patient's mental condition. In some cases, emotional stress may activate or irritate an ulcer. Even when an ulcer is not involved, doctors are concerned with each patient's mental health. They know that stress, either physical or emotional, can lead to physical problems. If a patient appears to suffer from mental stress, a doctor may refer him or her to a specialist who could diagnose the patient's mental condition.

Physicians estimate that the history contributes approximately 75% of the information needed to make a diagnosis. Recording the history is a well-established tradition in medical practice. The renowned Greek healer Hippocrates took case histories so complete and detailed that 2,000 years later, many of his patients can be diagnosed solely on the basis of these histories.

THE PHYSICAL EXAM

During the physical examination, doctors take advantage of two resources: their training, which has taught them to look for specific traits and abnormalities, and their senses of sight, hearing, touch, and smell. A physical examination also follows a logical sequence in which the physician studies the body in thorough, organized steps. The procedure begins with the doctor checking height, weight, pulse, and blood pressure. He or she then follows an orderly process that begins with the head, proceeds down to the chest, moves to the abdominal region, and finally examines the pelvic area.

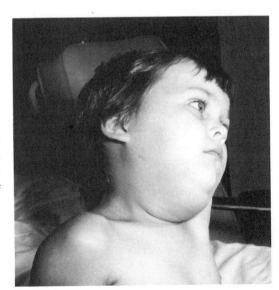

The first step of the physical examination involves inspection, during which the doctor looks for outward signs of an illness. To a trained eye, this child has an obvious case of the mumps.

Inspection

The first step in the exam is called the *inspection*. Simply by looking at various parts of the patient's body, the doctor can often make a successful diagnosis. This ability is especially useful in cases of diseases and conditions that produce recognizable alterations in a person's physical appearance. For instance, the disease *acromegaly* causes enlargement of the hands, feet, jaws, and nose. Another example is *Bell's palsy*, which prevents a patient from closing the eye, smiling, or showing the teeth on the side of the face affected by the disease.

The eyes, skin, chest, and abdomen also provide diagnostic clues when inspected closely. A doctor often can plainly see an enlarged stomach or spleen, or a tumor in the abdominal area. Taking the pulse is also part of the inspection. Different pulse rates are associated

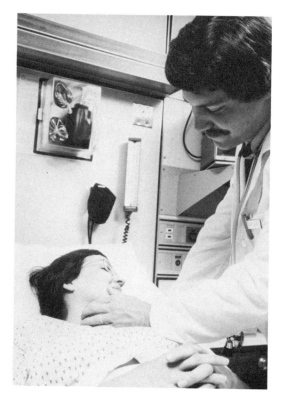

In palpation, the doctor uses his or her fingers to check for symptoms such as tenderness, bone fractures, and fluid buildup.

with different conditions, and an abnormally high or low pulse rate can steer a doctor's diagnosis in a specific direction.

Palpation

The next step in the exam is called *palpation*, which involves examining the patient with the fingers and hands. During this procedure, the doctor either confirms what was seen in the inspection or searches for further clues to the patient's problem. During palpation, the physician presses or squeezes certain parts of the body to learn whether they are tender or painful. Tenderness and pain are often signs of known conditions. For instance, tenderness in the area of the appendix can be a sign of appendicitis.

Listening through a stethoscope, a physician can use percussion to help determine if the lungs contain fluid or if the heart or other organs are abnormally large.

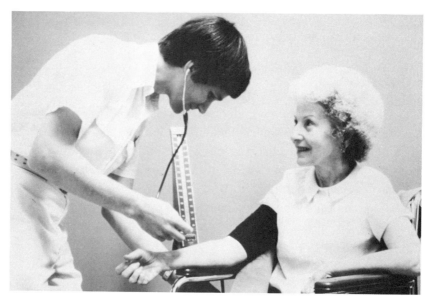

A physical exam often involves taking various measurements, such as weight, temperature, and blood pressure. Abnormally high blood pressure may signal serious heart and circulatory problems.

The doctor also looks for other effects produced by touching. For example, *edema*, or fluid buildup, in the ankles is revealed when the doctor presses on the skin, leaving an impression of the finger that persists for several seconds. Palpation is also valuable in diagnosing bone fractures and abnormalities that sometimes can be felt easily through the skin.

Percussion

Percussion, or tapping with the fingers, plays an important part in the physical exam. Listening through a stethoscope, a doctor can detect fluid in the lungs, help determine the position and size of the heart, and listen for signs of abnormal enlargement of the liver, stomach, or spleen.

To determine the size of the liver, for example, the physician begins by tapping above the bowel, which is filled with air. The tapping produces a characteristic hollow sound. The examiner proceeds higher until a dull sound is heard, denoting the lower border of the liver. The examiner marks this point on the patient's skin with a special pen. Next, percussion is applied to the lower lung area, which also has a distinct hollow sound. Working downward, the examiner hears a dull sound corresponding to the upper border of the liver. After this point is marked, the examiner measures the distance between the marks to determine the liver's size.

Other Measurements

Because certain ailments produce abnormally high or low temperatures, a thermometer reading may allow a physician to rule out certain conditions and draw attention to others. Similarly, by taking the patient's blood pressure, the doctor discovers more clues. Serious heart and circulatory conditions, for instance, are often signalled by abnormally high blood pressure.

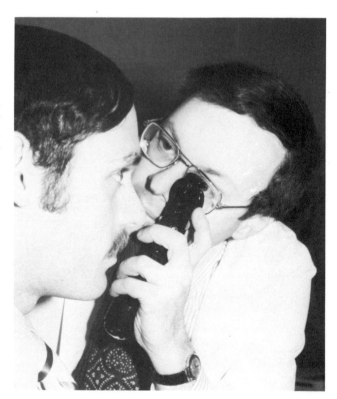

An ophthalmoscope enables a doctor to examine the retina and other eye areas. Abnormal blood vessels or bleeding in the eye may suggest the presence of a certain condition or disease.

Depending on the patient's appearance and what the doctor determines from the medical history and initial touching and listening, the physical exam may require further steps. The doctor might use an ophthalmoscope to look at the retina and other parts of the eye. This instrument can reveal abnormal-looking blood vessels or bleeding in the eye, which are symptomatic of various diseases and conditions. The physician often checks the eardrums for swelling or puncture and looks down the throat to search for signs of infection or problems in the tonsils or larynx.

Although they are not perfect, the history and physical examination remain the most important tools for making a diagnosis. They offer the most essential clues to a patient's condition and give the doctor a picture of the patient's health. This overview enables the physician to make a firm diagnosis or raise questions for further investigation. If the doctor cannot firmly diagnose the patient's problem after these procedures, additional tests may be necessary.

CHAPTER 4

MODERN DIAGNOSTIC TESTING

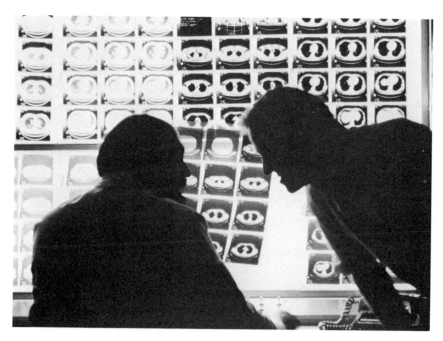

Administering and reading the results of a lab test often involve the expertise of a trained specialist who consults with the patient's primary physician before a diagnosis is made.

After a doctor has completed an initial examination of the patient, it may be necessary to follow up with one or more diagnostic procedures using special instruments, machines, or methods that are collectively called *diagnostic tests*. These range from the microscopic examination of body fluids or tissues to the insertion of tubes into the body to scrutinize it from the inside.

At this stage a doctor must decide which test will best answer his or her questions concerning the patient's condition. The doctor must also decide whether a certain test is safe for the patient. For instance, if the doctor suspects that the patient has *hepatitis*, a disease of the liver, it may be unsafe to perform a *biopsy*, a procedure that removes tissue from the liver for study under a microscope. In such a case, the doctor could order other tests that would not require the removal of tissue to confirm his or her suspicion, and thus decrease the risk of injuring the liver itself.

After testing is performed, the physician must consider four factors in order to analyze test results. First, the physician must know the specific condition that the test was designed to measure. For instance, a test for cancerous tissue in a particular organ may show whether cancer is present but may not indicate an alternative cause of illness if cancer is absent. Second, the doctor must consider how accurate the measurement was. If the results were inconclusive or in some way unclear, a second test might need to be ordered.

The third factor in analyzing a test is the doctor's knowledge. He or she must know normal measurements within the patient's general class of size, sex, and age. For example, if an adult male is tested for diabetes, the doctor considers what the average measurements of blood sugar are for adult males and judges the results of the test accordingly. High levels of sugar in the man's blood would indicate that his cells are not breaking down the sugar that his body needs for proper functioning. Finally, the physician must consider the definite statements that can be made from studying the test results. These conclusions usually confirm or deny the doctor's initial suspicions.

X RAYS

One of the most common diagnostic instruments used today is the X-ray machine. The principle behind this method is quite simple: X rays have a shorter wavelength than visible light has, a quality that allows them to pass through most materials. Dense objects, such as bone, allow only a few X rays through and therefore appear as white shadows on an X ray. On the other hand, less dense materials, such as

Developed in the 1970s, computerized axial tomography (CT scan) can help diagnose abnormalities in the brain. While a patient lies down, a rotating scanner sends information to a computer that creates an image.

air and living tissue, permit X rays to penetrate and thus show up as darker shadows on an X ray. Doctors and X-ray technicians are trained to differentiate various internal organs and structures when studying an X-ray image.

Angiogram

X rays are most often used to diagnose broken bones and to analyze problems in the lungs and abdomen. Yet many other X-ray procedures are designed to view specific areas and parts of the body. For example, if a doctor wants to check for abnormalities in the arteries of the lungs, heart, kidneys, or other organs, an *angiogram* might be necessary. Blood vessels usually cannot be seen on normal X rays, but an angiogram makes use of a special dye that is injected into the patient's blood system. When X rays are taken, the dye distinctly outlines the vessels, so the doctor can detect such problems as blood clots in the lungs, cancerous tumors surrounded by blood vessels, or vessels that are the source of a bleeding ulcer.

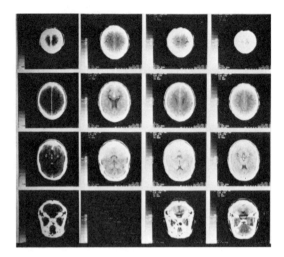

CT scans produce a complicated type of X ray. A computer that generates three-dimensional images enables doctors to view the brain at several angles simultaneously.

Computerized Axial Tomography

A more complicated kind of X-ray technique, developed in the 1970s, is called *computerized axial tomography*, or the *CT scan*. Although CT scans are used to diagnose many medical problems, they are particularly useful for studying brain abnormalities. To administer a CT scan to the brain, a technician has the patient lie down on a special table, then places a circular device around the patient's head.

The circular device, called a *scanner*, surrounds the head like a sort of box and takes X rays of the head from several different angles simultaneously. A detector records the numerous X rays and converts the information into electrical signals that are sent to a computer. The computer combines the signals and creates a three-dimensional picture of the patient's head. The doctor can then view this image on a TV screen. This method has proved extremely effective for revealing brain tumors and areas of the brain damaged by stroke.

MAGNETIC RESONANCE IMAGING

One of the newest methods used for diagnosis is *magnetic resonance imaging*. It involves a gigantic cylindrical magnet that may weigh as much as 100 tons, and thus this process is usually found only in hospitals. The patient lies inside the device while this painless test is performed.

The test is based on the principle that the body contains particles called *protons* that align themselves to a magnetic field, such as that of the machine. After the machine's magnetic pull is turned off, the particles return to their previous position, a movement that releases energy at measurable frequencies. These frequencies are fed into a computer that creates a precise picture of the body's inner activity.

Magnetic resonance imaging can also be used to produce pictures of the body's movement, so it becomes easier to pinpoint the source of pain in a moving body part such as a joint. The test seems most useful for finding abnormalities in the brain, spinal cord, bones, heart, and other organs. It identifies internal swelling that is often related to brain infections and tumors but appears less effective than CT scans at differentiating between early swelling and small tumors.

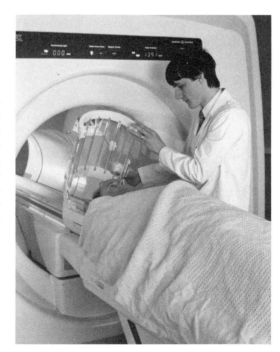

During magnetic resonance imaging (MRI) of the brain, the large coils of a magnet surround the patient's head. The smaller device receives the frequencies that the body produces in response to the magnet's pull.

Ultrasound, a test that is often used to check for problems of the heart or of the female reproductive tract, bounces sound waves off the inside of the body in order to produce visual images.

ULTRASOUND

Ultrasound, as its name implies, is based on principles that apply to sound. Because the procedure is painless and safe, it has become very popular as a way to obtain images of the inside of the body. The test is particularly useful for diagnosing heart disease and problems in the female reproductive tract.

An ultrasound is performed after a special jelly is rubbed over the area to be tested. Then a scanner is passed over the area and measures vibrations as they bounce off the body's internal areas. These vibrations have the same physical properties of sound, but because their frequencies are above a range that humans can hear they are recorded with a special device. Recent developments have used this method to produce colored images of the inside of blood vessels.

MICROBIOLOGY

Microbiology is the study of microorganisms, or germs. The diagnostic test used to detect the presence of dangerous microorganisms is called a *culture*. If a doctor suspects that his or her patient has a urinary tract infection, pneumonia, *strep throat*, a sexually transmitted disease, or some other condition caused by a microorganism, he or she will order a culture.

To test for microorganisms, a nurse takes a sample of blood, spinal fluid, urine, or tissue and places it in a jellylike substance contained in a small dish. The culture is usually kept at body temperature (98.6 degrees Fahrenheit) and left to sit for 24 to 72 hours. During this time, the microorganisms multiply, providing a large enough sample for a technician to examine and identify the type of germs present. If harmful germs appear in the culture, the test is termed *positive*. No growth indicates that no harmful microorganisms were found, a *negative* result.

BLOOD TESTS

Another common diagnostic procedure is the blood test. Dozens of types of blood tests exist. Most involve drawing blood from the patient's arm and analyzing the sample through a microscope or by chemical or mechanical procedures. Each type of blood test reveals specific information about the patient's physical condition.

To determine whether harmful microorganisms or viruses are present in the body, medical technicians take a sample of bodily fluid or tissue. To analyze it, they use a microscope or other chemical or mechanical methods.

Some blood tests reveal the presence of certain drugs, including alcohol, in the bloodstream. Others measure the levels of essential chemicals and vitamins or determine the presence of dangerous diseases, such as syphilis or sickle cell anemia. A *glucose tolerance test* specifically measures the levels of *glucose*, or natural sugar, in the blood. If these levels are too high, the patient may have diabetes; if abnormally low, the patient may have *hypoglycemia*.

URINE AND STOOL TESTS

Urine tests are very useful for diagnosing a number of different diseases and conditions. The urine's color alone may suggest certain problems. For instance, brownish yellow urine is often a sign of hepatitis. The clarity of the urine is also a clue. Cloudy or milky urine might indicate the presence of bacteria from a urinary tract infection.

Dipstick analysis is a urine-testing procedure that uses strips of plastic coated with chemicals. When these are dipped into a urine sample, the chemicals react with various substances in the urine, turning the strips different colors. The doctor or laboratory technician is trained to recognize that certain colors indicate the presence of specific substances in the urine.

For example, the dipstick procedure can be used to test for *ketones*, by-products produced when the body burns fat. If the analysis shows that ketones are present, the doctor might suspect malnutrition, starvation, prolonged vomiting, or diabetes. Dipstick tests also measure the acidity of the urine. Highly *alkaline* (low in acidity) urine, for example, is a sign of kidney disease. Urine tests also measure levels of such substances as vitamins, minerals, hormones, and drugs.

Lab tests performed on the *stool*, or excrement, are important for detecting diseases or other problems in the bowels, intestines, and organs. For example, a stool that is tan or white might indicate a blockage of the passages leading from the liver or gall bladder, a sign of hepatitis, gallstones, or cancer. A stool that is mixed with blood or pus can indicate that the patient has colitis, an inflammation of the *colon*, or large intestine. A high fat content is sometimes a sign of disease in the pancreas. Other stool tests reveal the presence of harm-

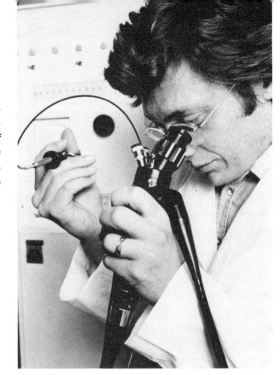

During endoscopy, a specialist uses a tube with a laser light attached to look inside the body. Many of these tubes have a microscope at the doctor's end to ease diagnosis.

ful bacteria that cause diseases such as cholera and typhoid, as well as parasites such as hookworm, tapeworm, and pinworm.

ENDOSCOPY

Endoscopy is the general name given to a number of diagnostic procedures involving the insertion of tubes with attached light sources into various parts of the body. The doctor, almost always a specialist trained in a specific endoscopic procedure, looks through a thin, flexible tube that enables light to bend as the tube moves through the body's passages.

A lens mounted to the outer end of this thin tube enables the doctor to see many of the internal organs and other body parts. The end of the tube that explores the inside of the body may also contain a microscope, to give the doctor a closer look. Tiny instruments may also be inserted through the tube and pieces of tissue collected for laboratory study. Such procedures allow doctors to gather diagnostic information that was once obtainable only through exploratory operations.

Arthroscopy is a type of endoscopy in which the doctor looks into the joints between the bones, especially those in the knee, shoulder, and ankle. When a knee injury occurs, for instance, the doctor may suspect damage to the ligaments or cartilage in the joint area. After the application of a local *anesthetic* (a drug that produces numbness), a small incision is made in the side of the leg, and a thin tube, called an *arthroscope*, is inserted into the joint. If the doctor sees torn tissue, he or she can sometimes remove it directly through the tube, making surgery unnecessary. Arthroscopy, which usually takes about an hour, can also be used to diagnose arthritic damage in the joints.

Bronchoscopy is a common form of endoscopy that explores problems in the breathing passages and lungs. Diseases that affect the chest area, such as TB and lung cancer, do not always show up clearly on X rays, so doctors often call for bronchoscopy when an X ray reveals an indistinct abnormality in the lungs.

In this procedure, a *bronchoscope* is used to view the insides of the *bronchi*, or bronchial tubes, which feed air from the *trachea*, or windpipe, into the air sacs of the lungs. Most often, the patient is completely anesthetized before the bronchoscope is inserted through the mouth or nose. A sample of tissue can be taken by a tiny cutting instrument inserted through the tube.

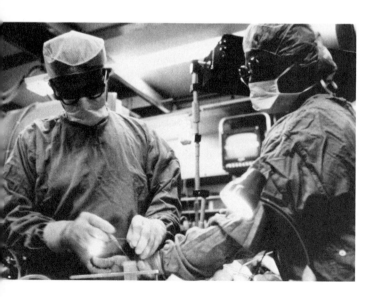

In some cases, lasers are used to make a diagnosis and administer treatment in the same procedure. During bronchoscopy, a laser's light may reveal an unhealthy growth in the lungs; the laser's heat can then be intensified to burn away the unwanted growth.

Other types of endoscopy include *upper gastrointestinal endoscopy*, used to examine the esophagus and stomach, *gastroscopy*, used to study the stomach and small intestine, and *colonoscopy*, used to view the interior of the colon. Certain endoscopic procedures are particularly helpful in diagnosing women's illnesses, including *hysteroscopy*, in which doctors examine the cervix and uterus, and *laparoscopy*, in which they view the abdominal and pelvic areas.

OTHER TESTS

Sometimes doctors must remove tissue from the body to study it further. A biopsy is performed by scraping or cutting off a sample of tissue and then examining it under a microscope. If the tissue is in any way abnormal, the doctor either makes a diagnosis based on this finding or orders further tests to confirm the results of the biopsy.

One way of performing a biopsy is to take samples during endoscopy. The other, more common, approach is to insert a hollow needle through the skin and then suction tissue from an organ. Conditions that are commonly diagnosed using biopsies are kidney failure, cancer, and cirrhosis.

A *Pap smear* is a test for diagnosing cancer of the *cervix*, the narrow outer end of the uterus. Cervical cancer is one of the most common cancers in women. At one time it almost always proved fatal because it was rarely discovered early enough to treat successfully. The Pap smear, which allows early detection, was named after Dr. George Papanicolaou, who developed it in 1948. By the 1950s, Pap smears became routine preventive procedures and are now administered to healthy women once every one to three years.

To perform a Pap smear, the doctor carefully scrapes a small sample of tissue from the cervix and applies the sample to a microscope slide. A lab technician then examines the tissue for any dangerous or cancerous cells. If the test is positive, usually the cancer has been detected in its early stages and can be eliminated through surgery or other procedures.

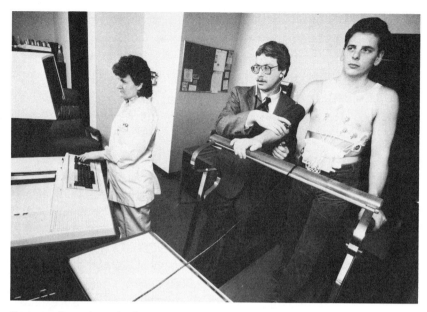

The cardiac stress test measures the heart's reaction to strain. The electrodes taped to the patient's chest send signals to the electro- cardiograph machine (left), which prints the heart's impulses on a moving sheet of paper.

Other common tests used in medical diagnosis are the *sweat test*, which detects *cystic fibrosis* (a disease that alters chemicals in the glands, affecting the ability to breathe, perspire, and eat), the *mammogram*, which tests for breast cancer, and the *audiogram*, which reveals and measures hearing loss.

DIAGNOSTIC TOOLS

The *electrocardiogram*, referred to as an *EKG*, is used to diagnose heart disease by tracing changes in the electrical impulses emitted by the heart. These impulses cause the heart to contract regularly and to pump blood. This constant electrical activity can be detected by placing small metal electrodes on the skin of the wrists, ankles, and chest. Wires connect these electrodes to an *electrocardiograph*, a machine that prints the heart's impulses as a pattern on a moving sheet of paper. This tracing of the heart's changes shows any abnormalities in the heart's action, an indicator of heart disease.

Doctors are trained to recognize EKG patterns corresponding to normal electrical activity in the heart. When something is wrong with the organ, its electrical activity changes, registering abnormal impulses on the EKG. Conditions such as heart attack, irregular heartbeats, heart enlargement, rheumatic fever, and decreased oxygen supply to the heart can be detected by this reliable diagnostic method.

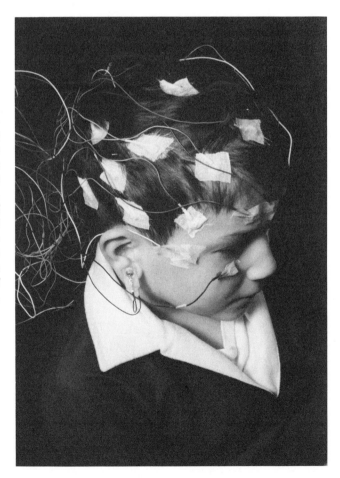

The electro-encephalogram uses electrodes taped to the patient's head to measure the brain's electrical impulses. Specialists are trained to interpret abnormal patterns of brain activity that may indicate stroke, epilepsy, or the presence of a blood clot or tumor.

Another useful diagnostic tool is the *electroencephalogram*, called an *EEG*, which is a measure of electrical impulses in the brain. Electrodes attached to the skin of the head feed brain impulses into the EEG machine, which reveals either normal or abnormal patterns of brain activity. This approach is routinely used to diagnose illnesses of the brain, such as tumors, stroke, epilepsy, infection, and blood clots.

Coma and brain death are also diagnosed with the EEG. A patient is considered brain-dead when all electrical activity in the brain has stopped, even if the heart continues beating. In states that officially define death as brain death, doctors are often called upon to provide evidence that brain activity has ceased. An EEG offers proof that a patient can be removed legally from life-support machinery.

CHAPTER 5

MAKING THE DIAGNOSIS

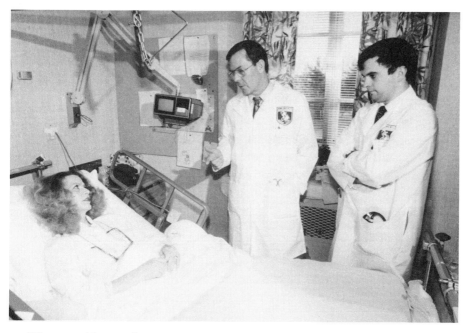

When making a diagnosis, physicians consider all of the available information. They then list it in an order based on which facts seem most important in analyzing an illness.

After collecting the facts about a patient's condition by studying his or her history, conducting a physical exam, and ordering any necessary lab procedures, the doctor must next analyze the results. To do so, the physician first lists the information in order of importance.

Consider, for instance, a patient who complains of a prolonged and painful sore throat. The patient's history may reveal a broken leg and the removal of the appendix 30 years before. However, the doctor logically will place these problems at the bottom of the list, as they have no connection to the patient's present problem. On the other hand, the patient's smoking habit should be placed higher on the list because smoking can cause or further irritate a sore throat. Results of tests run by the doctor, such as a strep throat culture, will be placed at the top of the list of important facts. (Strep throat is a throat infection caused by the *streptococcus* bacteria.)

Once the information has been arranged properly, the doctor looks for one fact that, in and of itself, will provide the diagnosis. For example, if the strep throat culture in the previous example is positive, the doctor will not need to make any further considerations. The straightforward diagnosis will be strep throat, and the doctor will prescribe treatment accordingly.

Often, however, the diagnosis is more complicated. If, for instance, the strep throat culture is negative, the doctor must choose among several other possible causes for an inflamed, painful throat. Perhaps

Lab tests often provide the most significant clues to the cause of disease. Doctors must know the appropriate test to administer for each condition and then interpret the results.

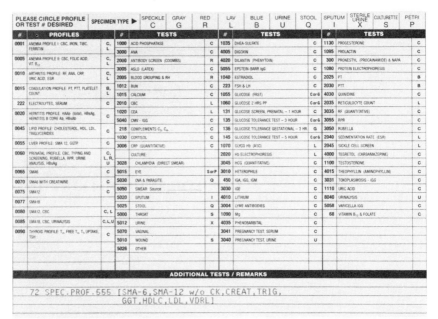

PLEASE CIRCLE PROFILE OR TEST # DESIRED	SPECIMEN TYPE ▶	SPECKLE C	GRAY G	RED R	LAV L	BLUE B	URINE U	STOOL Q	SPUTUM I	STERILE URINE X	CULTURETTE S	PETRI P

PROFILES

#	PROFILES	
0001	ANEMIA PROFILE I: CBC, IRON, TIBC, FERRITIN	C, L
0005	ANEMIA PROFILE II: CBC, FOLIC ACID, VIT B12	C, L
0010	ARTHRITIS PROFILE: RF, ANA, CRP, URIC ACID, ESR	C, L
0015	COAGULATION PROFILE: PT, PTT, PLATELET COUNT	B, L
222	ELECTROLYTES, SERUM	C
0020	HEPATITIS PROFILE: HAAb (total), HBsAg, HEPATITIS B CORE Ab, HBsAb	C
0045	LIPID PROFILE: CHOLESTEROL, HDL, LDL, TRIGLYCERIDES	C
0055	LIVER PROFILE: SMA 12, GGTP	C
0060	PRENATAL PROFILE: CBC, TYPING AND SCREENING, RUBELLA, RPR, URINE ANALYSIS, HBsAg	C, L, R, U
0065	SMA6	C
0070	SMAs WITH CREATININE	C
0075	SMA12	C
0077	SMA18	
0080	SMA12, CBC	C, L
0085	SMA18, CBC, URINALYSIS	C, L, U
0090	THYROID PROFILE T4, FREE T4, T3 UPTAKE, TSH	C

TESTS

#	TESTS	
1000	ACID PHOSPHATASE	C
3000	ANA	C
2000	ANTIBODY SCREEN (COOMBS)	R
3005	ASLO (LATEX)	C
2005	BLOOD GROUPING & RH	R
1012	BUN	C
1015	CALCIUM	C
2010	CBC	L
1020	CEA	L
5040	CMV - IGG	C
218	COMPLEMENTS C3, C4	C
1030	CORTISOL	C
3006	CRP (QUANTITATIVE)	C
	CULTURE	
3028	CHLAMYDIA (DIRECT SMEAR)	
5015	EYE	S or P
5030	OVA & PARASITE	Q
5050	SMEAR Source	
5020	SPUTUM	I
5025	STOOL	Q
5000	THROAT	S
5012	URINE	X
5070	VAGINAL	
5010	WOUND	S
5026	OTHER	

#	TESTS	
1035	DHEA-SULFATE	C
4005	DIGOXIN	C
4020	DILANTIN (PHENYTOIN)	C
5055	EPSTEIN-BARR IgG	C
1040	ESTRADIOL	C
223	FSH & LH	C
1055	GLUCOSE (FAST)	C or 6
1060	GLUCOSE 2 HRS PP	L
131	GLUCOSE SCREEN, PRENATAL - 1 HOUR	C
135	GLUCOSE TOLERANCE TEST - 3 HOUR	C or 6
136	GLUCOSE TOLERANCE GESTATIONAL - 3 HR	G
145	GLUCOSE TOLERANCE TEST - 5 HOUR	C or 6
1070	GLYCO Hb (A1C)	L
2020	Hb ELECTROPHORESIS	L
3045	HCG (QUANTITATIVE)	C
3010	HETEROPHILE	C
450	IGA, IGG, IGM	C
3030	IGE	C
4010	LITHIUM	C
3004	LYME ANTIBODIES	C
1090	Mg	C
4035	PHENOBARBITAL	C
3041	PREGNANCY TEST, SERUM	C
3040	PREGNANCY TEST, URINE	U

#	TESTS	
1130	PROGESTERONE	C
1095	PROLACTIN	C
300	PRONESTYL (PROCAINAMIDE) & NAPA	C
1080	PROTEIN ELECTROPHORESIS	C
2025	PT	B
2030	PTT	B
4030	QUINIDINE	C
2035	RETICULOCYTE COUNT	L
3035	RF (QUANTITATIVE)	C
3055	RPR	C
3050	RUBELLA	C
2040	SEDIMENTATION RATE (ESR)	L
2045	SICKLE CELL SCREEN	L
4000	TEGRETOL (CARBAMAZEPINE)	C
1100	TESTOSTERONE	C
4015	THEOPHYLLIN (AMINOPHYLLIN)	C
3031	TOXOPLASMOSIS - IGG	C
1110	URIC ACID	C
8040	URINALYSIS	U
5058	VARICELLA IGG	C
68	VITAMIN B12 & FOLATE	C

ADDITIONAL TESTS / REMARKS

72 SPEC.PROF.555 [SMA-6,SMA-12 w/o CK,CREAT,TRIG, GGT,HDLC,LDL,VDRL]

a test was also done for *thrush*, an infection of the throat caused by a fungus. If that test was negative, a number of other possibilities still remain.

The doctor must now search through other facts for some symptom or sign of the condition that will help identify the cause of the patient's sore throat. Symptoms such as headache and fever might be the clues the doctor needs. Piecing the important facts together, the doctor may conclude that the patient has a case of the flu. This diagnosis may be especially logical if there has been a recent local outbreak of a new flu strain.

DIAGNOSING COMMON CONDITIONS

An examination of some actual cases further illustrates the process that physicians follow to make diagnoses.

Circulatory Problems

Jack A., a 35-year-old serviceman, went to see a doctor after experiencing periodic episodes of *dyspnea* (shortness of breath) and pains in the chest. Jack's history revealed that he had undergone an appendectomy two years earlier. Just two weeks after the operation, he first noticed the chest pains, which were often accompanied by dyspnea and heavy sweats. One year later, Jack endured an episode of dyspnea so severe that he feared he would die of suffocation. A day or two later, after running up the stairs, he became dizzy and fainted.

Eventually, he experienced swelling in both legs. When he finally visited the doctor a year later, the doctor admitted Jack to the hospital for extensive tests. The physician reasoned that the chest pains and swelling in the legs were signs that Jack's heart and circulatory system were not working properly. One possibility was that an obstruction, called an *embolism*, was periodically blocking some of Jack's blood vessels and temporarily reducing the normal blood flow. *Emboli* are small abnormal particles that float through the bloodstream, often after dislodging from one of various parts of the body. Jack's EKG showed that his heart was beating abnormally in a way that is often the result of such obstructions.

Jack's episodes of dyspnea, sweating, and fainting also pointed to the presence of emboli in the bloodstream. When blood flow in the veins is reduced because of blockage, the exchange of oxygen and carbon dioxide in the lungs is affected, and shortness of breath can result. As the body works harder to adjust to the abnormal situation, perspiration increases. Because the blockage in the veins impedes the flow of blood, any unusual exertion that requires increased blood flow can have serious consequences. One such consequence can be a reduction in the normal amount of blood flowing toward the brain. This oxygen reduction, the doctor reasoned, accounted for Jack's fainting after running up the stairs.

Another fact the doctor considered was the swelling in Jack's legs. Swelling can have a number of different causes. One of these is an uneven flow of blood through the veins as a result of blockage. Thus, when combined with the other symptoms, the swelling appeared to further confirm the presence of emboli in the blood vessels.

Unfortunately, while further tests were being run, Jack had a sudden heart attack and died. The *autopsy*, an examination performed after death, revealed that the doctor's suspicions had been correct. Jack had suffered from a blockage of the blood vessels due to blood clots. One of these clots eventually became lodged in one of the openings of his heart, temporarily upsetting the flow of blood through the heart and causing his death. Jack suffered from a common circulatory problem encountered regularly in hospitals. If he had gone to a doctor earlier, modern diagnostic techniques could have recommended treatment in time to save his life.

Diabetes

Nancy M., a young housewife, had another common health problem, although she was not aware of its source. All she knew was that she had been feeling ill for some time and had put off seeking medical help. Eventually her illness began to disrupt her life, so she went to see her doctor.

This diabetic boy is measuring the level of sugar in his blood. The self-administered test should be used to monitor appropriate sugar levels only after a doctor officially diagnoses a person as diabetic.

During the initial examination, the doctor noted Nancy's symptoms. She often suffered from fatigue and felt weak and lethargic. Sometimes she lost weight, even though her food intake remained the same. Nancy also complained of unusually frequent urination and excessive thirst. In addition, she said, her friends had recently accused her of being grouchy and hard to get along with.

Nancy's doctor immediately recognized her symptoms as classic signs of diabetes, a serious disease that affects millions of people around the world. The doctor explained to Nancy how her symptoms clearly reflected the nature of the disease. The cells of diabetics, he said, have trouble absorbing and breaking down the glucose from food.

Glucose is an important carbohydrate that cells need for healthy functioning. For people with diabetes, much of the sugar that should be absorbed by the cells accumulates in the bloodstream, raising blood sugar levels. Because so many of Nancy's cells were starved for sugar, the doctor explained, she often felt tired and weak. And because her cells were receiving less of their needed carbohydrates, she also experienced some weight loss.

Epidemics Throughout History

THE BLACK DEATH

In 1347, the Mongols besieged the Italian colony of Kaffa on the northern coast of the Black Sea. The attackers catapulted the bodies of disease victims into the town, hoping to infect and weaken the defenders. The victims, members of the Mongol army, had died of a strange disease that had originated somewhere in central Asia. The affliction struck quickly, causing swelling in the groin and armpits, dark splotches on the skin, terrible pain, and finally death. Eventually, so many of the Mongol soldiers died of the disease, they had to abandon the seige.

Even so, Kaffa did not escape decimation, because many of the residents were infected by this early form of biological warfare. The bacterial source of the disease infected fleas, which in turn infected the rats they infested. Humans either caught the disease from the rats and fleas or from each other.

The disease began to spread through Italy. Ships carried infected rats and humans to the cities of Genoa and Venice, and to Messina on the island of Sicily. From these towns, the plague, which became known as the *black death*, traveled swiftly across Europe. Estimates for the death toll in the 3 years following the initial outbreak range from 20 to 30 million, at least one-third of the population of Europe.

Fear of catching the disease was so intense that the structure of social and family life often broke down. Writing in Florence, the poet Giovanni Boccaccio (1313–75) commented, "Such terror was struck into the hearts of men and women by this calamity that brother abandoned brother, and the uncle his nephew, and sister her brother, and very often the wife her husband. What is even worse and nearly incredible is that fathers and mothers refused to see and tend their children, as if they had not been theirs."

INFLUENZA

In the fall of 1918 in Washington, D.C., a distraught young woman telephoned local authorities to

Soldiers wear face masks to protect themselves from a deadly strain of flu that appeared at the end of World War I.

report that two of her roommates had died and that the other was sick. The police paid a visit to the house two days later and found the caller and the fourth roommate both dead from influenza.

The tragic discovery was all too familiar. The disease, caused by a virus and displaying symptoms similar to those of pneumonia, had been spreading with amazing speed that year, killing Americans at a rate of more than 1,000 per day. On October 23, 1918, 851 people died of influenza in New York City alone. Ultimately, more than 550,000 Americans are estimated to have succumbed to this outbreak, almost 10 times the number of men the United States lost in battle during World War I.

It was in the final months of that war, in the spring of 1918, that a particularly deadly strain of influenza virus swept through army camps in Europe, striking down thousands of Allied and German soldiers. Surviving troops carried the disease back to their respective countries, where it spread unchecked.

Scientists and doctors had not yet isolated and studied viruses, so they could not identify the cause of the outbreak or how to stop it. People desperately tried all sorts of home remedies, consuming huge amounts of garlic, having teeth and tonsils removed, and inhaling *chloroform*, a powerful anesthetic. All attempts to cure or slow the spread of the disease failed.

Eventually the worldwide epidemic, or *pandemic*, ran its course and the death toll decreased. Although other strains of influenza have killed thousands of people in epidemics each year since, the 1918 pandemic remains the worst outbreak on record. In addition to the heavy loss of life in the United States, more than half a million people died in Mexico; 450,000 in Russia; and 375,000 in Italy, with the pandemic's global death toll exceeding 20 million.

Glucose must pass through the kidneys before it is excreted from the body, so the more glucose the body contains, the more water is needed by the kidneys to aid in this process. Therefore, a great deal of water was drawn from Nancy's tissues, and the result was more frequent urination. Because that lost water had to be replaced, she felt thirsty and drank excessive amounts of water. The doctor was not surprised that her friends found her hard to get along with. He explained that irritability is another common symptom of diabetes, as are itchy skin, blurred vision, and poor healing of cuts.

To confirm his initial diagnosis, Nancy's doctor ordered a glucose tolerance test. After fasting for several hours, she drank a solution containing a measured amount of glucose and, once an hour for three hours, gave a nurse samples of her blood and urine. A lab examined these samples and observed how her blood sugar levels changed. The test confirmed that Nancy was diabetic, and the doctor immediately initiated treatment.

DIAGNOSING INFECTIOUS DISEASES

In addition to dealing with conditions that interrupt the body's proper functions, doctors must regularly diagnose *infectious*, or contagious, diseases. These illnesses spread from person to person by microor-

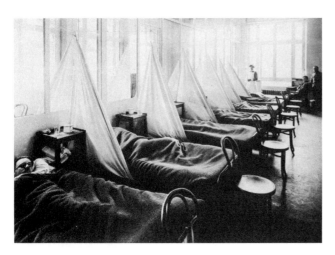

Influenza, perhaps the world's most commonly encountered epidemic, killed millions in the early 20th century. These American soldiers, in a U.S. army base in France, are recovering from the influenza epidemic that followed World War I.

ganisms such as bacteria and infectious agents such as viruses. Examination of tissue or blood samples under a microscope usually provides a firm and accurate diagnosis, because the microorganisms of most diseases show clear and characteristic shapes and behaviors. Outwardly, each infectious disease produces certain recognizable symptoms, although two or more diseases may exhibit very similar symptoms.

Swift and correct diagnosis of contagious diseases is important, not only to provide effective treatment for the patient but also to prevent these diseases from spreading to others. Quick diagnosis is especially important for certain diseases that have repeatedly reached epidemic proportions. Two of these cases are examined below.

Influenza

Influenza killed millions of people worldwide in the early years of the 20th century and continues to kill thousands of people each year. Therefore, doctors must be able to recognize the symptoms of influenza, a task made difficult because its symptoms are similar to those of other diseases. To complicate matters, one type of illness, *bacterial*

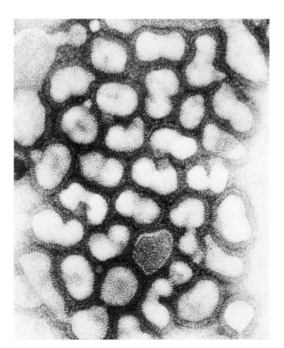

Many diseases are easily recognized once they are examined through a microscope. This micrograph of the influenza virus is enhanced by a powerful electron microscope.

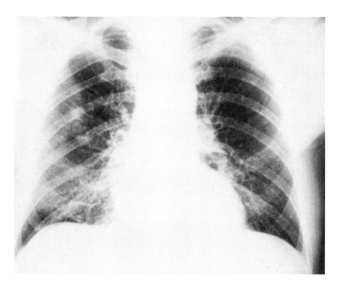

Certain diseases, such as influenza, hinder a correct diagnosis because their symptoms resemble those of a different illness. This X ray offers distinct evidence that pneumonia is present, although the problem first appeared to be influenza.

pneumonia, often develops in the wake of an influenza attack, so a doctor can be fooled into thinking that only influenza is present.

The problems involved in diagnosing influenza can be better understood by considering how the disease develops. Influenza is an infection of the lungs and upper respiratory tract caused by any of a wide variety of influenza viruses. The disease strikes very suddenly with symptoms such as chills, headache, pains in the back and legs, very high fever, dry throat, nasal congestion, and severe cough. These symptoms are very similar to those of various types of pneumonia, many of which are caused by bacteria. The symptoms of other conditions, including strep throat and ear infections, can also be confused with those of influenza.

Often, the influenza viruses damage the delicate membranes of the lungs, leaving them open to further infection by pneumonia bacteria such as streptococci. The combination of viral influenza and bacterial pneumonia can be physically devastating and accounts for the high death rate in influenza epidemics. Yet certain laboratory microbiology tests can reveal the presence of bacterial pneumonia; if these tests are not performed, however, the doctor may diagnose influenza only, and the treatment may be ineffective.

Bubonic plague, which afflicted millions in previous centuries, appears so rarely today that modern doctors barely recognize it. Yet in 1900, San Francisco's Chinese community battled an attack of plague that spread throughout Chinatown.

Bubonic Plague

Certain diseases are so rare that they become difficult to diagnose by doctors who never expect to encounter them. If the disease is rare and the doctor performing the examination is not familiar with the symptoms, arriving at the correct diagnosis may take several hours or even several days. During that time, the patient's condition could become critical, or the disease could spread to other people.

One example of a rare disease is *bubonic plague*, often referred to simply as plague. Although it wiped out millions of people in past centuries, it occurs only rarely today. Few modern doctors have ever seen a case of plague, and those who do encounter it usually turn to lengthy lab tests or the advice of specialists in order to make a definite diagnosis.

Bubonic plague is caused by bacteria that, once inside the body, multiply rapidly, especially in the *lymph nodes*. These are the small bean-shaped organs located in the armpits, neck, groin, legs, and elsewhere that produce white blood cells to fight microorganisms and other foreign materials that invade the body. The plague bacteria cause the nodes to bleed and swell, forming dark lumps called *buboes*, for which the disease was named. If the buboes are small and inconspicuous, as is sometimes the case, an unsuspecting doctor might make the wrong diagnosis.

The plague bacteria also release *toxins*, or poisons, that can cause the collapse of the circulatory system, including the heart. Often, the bacteria spread into the lungs, causing infection and pneumonia. The victim then exhibits all the symptoms of pneumonia, including coughing, which spreads the disease by releasing tiny water droplets containing the bacteria into the air. Thus, plague affects many parts of the body, and some of its symptoms are the same as those of other diseases.

Although plague occurs infrequently, physicians do have one advantage when they encounter it: It is a known disease. Doctors and scientists understand how people get the plague and other better-known diseases and can make predictions about how they will affect the body. But occasionally new diseases appear that doctors know little or nothing about and for which no standard diagnoses exist. They present unsolved riddles that make diagnosis extremely difficult. Striving to understand these new and sometimes mysterious diseases is one of the great challenges faced by the science of medicine.

CHAPTER 6

DIAGNOSING NEW DISEASES

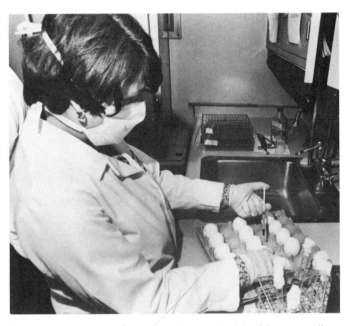

The art of diagnosis is put to its greatest test by new diseases. This microbiologist injects eggs with samples taken from people with an unknown illness in hopes that its microorganisms will grow plentiful enough to be detected.

Identifying diseases has been one of the most challenging aspects of medicine. The past century has brought doctors many solutions to much-sought-after medical riddles. However, new mysteries constantly present themselves. Although modern medical experts may be better able to find evidence, these clues do not always offer easy answers to these medical detectives. The efforts to identify and diagnose previously unseen diseases remain some of the greatest detective stories in history.

Although the methods and tools used in modern diagnosis have become very sophisticated, there is no guarantee that doctors will be able to detect and identify every disease they encounter. When medical personnel come across symptoms that do not match those of any known diseases, they begin to question whether a previously unknown disease has appeared—one that the medical community may not be prepared to fight.

In certain cases, doctors encounter new diseases that exhibit symptoms similar or identical to those of known illnesses. As a result, the problem may be misdiagnosed, and the physician may admister the wrong treatment. In extreme cases, this error could prove fatal.

In the 1970s and 1980s, three mysterious and debilitating diseases captured the attention of both the medical community and the public: *Legionnaires' disease, acquired immune deficiency syndrome* (AIDS), and *chronic fatigue syndrome* (CFS). The ways in which medical personnel first reacted to each of these conditions graphically illustrate the difficulties doctors face when confronting strange new diseases. Although the art of diagnosis always involves a bit of detective work, the ability of physicians to detect and analyze clues was severely tested by these three ailments.

The baffling attack of an unknown disease occurred during an American Legion convention in Philadelphia, Pennsylvania, in July 1976. Experts tested everyone attending the convention, naming the disease after its primary victims, Legionnaires.

LEGIONNAIRES' DISEASE

One night in July 1976, nearly 4,000 members of the American Legion attended a convention at a hotel in Philadelphia, Pennsylvania. What promised to be a pleasant, routine event ended up being neither. The next day, dozens of the Legionnaires were sick, and within 2 days, 220 of the people who had attended the meeting were deathly ill. All of the victims had similar symptoms: fever as high as 105°, severe dry cough, headache, chills, general weakness, and fatigue—all the symptoms normally associated with pneumonia.

The doctors who examined the Legionnaires ran standard lab tests looking for evidence of bacterial pneumonia, the most common form of the illness. When these tests came back negative, the doctors assumed the culprit was a virus, a microorganism much smaller and harder to detect than bacteria. As a result, the problem was diagnosed as viral pneumonia. Meanwhile, high fever and fluid in the lungs of the victims began to take their toll. Within a week, 34 of the people who had been at the Legion meeting had died of what had become known as Legionnaires' disease.

Many members of the Philadelphia medical community were disturbed, not only about the loss of life, but also about the strange

Based in Atlanta, Georgia, the Centers for Disease Control (CDC) is a federally funded institution that tracks the appearance and spread of diseases. It pays close attention to new and unusual symptoms, such as those reported in the Legionnaires' disease outbreak.

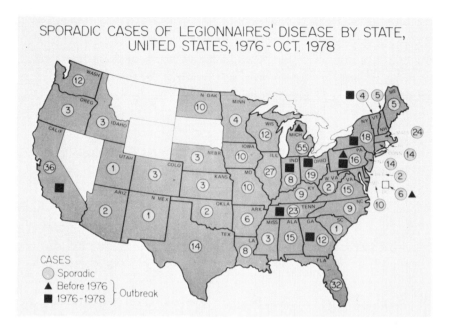

SPORADIC CASES OF LEGIONNAIRES' DISEASE BY STATE, UNITED STATES, 1976 - OCT. 1978

CASES
○ Sporadic
▲ Before 1976 ⎫ Outbreak
■ 1976-1978 ⎭

Following the 1976 outbreak of Legionnaires' disease, the CDC mapped its spread thoughout the United States. Accurate records will help doctors make speedy and successful diagnoses when future cases occur.

circumstances of this particular outbreak of pneumonia. Although viral pneumonia is extremely contagious, many doctors found it hard to believe that it could spread to more than 200 people in so short a time. Local doctors notified the Centers for Disease Control (CDC), a federal agency in Atlanta, Georgia, responsible for identifying and tracking the spread of infectious diseases reported in the United States. The CDC immediately sent investigators to Philadelphia.

The CDC investigators decided to concentrate their efforts on the source of the epidemic—the hotel where the convention was held. For five months, the search went on, focusing on the possibilities of poisons in the food, fungus spores spread through the air, and infection by various types of viruses and bacteria. The investigators eventually came to suspect that water droplets in the air from the building's cooling system contained microorganisms that caused the disease.

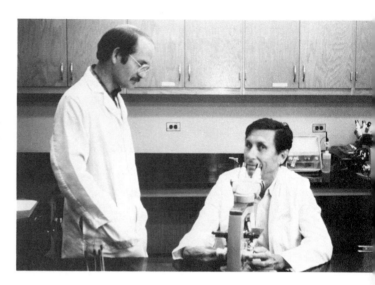

CDC microbiologist Joe McDade (left) with Charles Shepard (right), chief of the organization's Leprosy and Rickettsia Branch, used creative techniques to discover the tiny bacteria that turned out to be the cause of Legionnaires' disease.

At first, however, the investigators could not reconcile the clues with the cause: Viruses do not multiply in water supplies, and bacteria, which do, had not appeared in tests. Besides, the investigators reasoned, most bacteria do not thrive in cool, chlorinated water. Yet it appeared that some unknown disease agents that behaved like bacteria had caused the deaths.

Finally, a CDC microbiologist, Joe McDade, solved the mystery by using a nonstandard approach to laboratory diagnosis. He took samples of lung tissue from some of the infected people and injected the samples into guinea pigs. The animals quickly came down with the same symptoms displayed by the Legionnaires. McDade then injected tissue from the diseased guinea pigs into the yolk sacs of chicken embryos. Thus, if any hard-to-detect bacteria were present, they would grow in the warm, nutrient-rich sacs. Eventually, cultures of the invisible bacteria, called *legionella*, did appear under a powerful *electron microscope*, an instrument that uses a beam of electrons to reflect an enlarged image of a minute object.

Thus, McDade had proved that Legionnaires' disease was caused by unusual bacteria that somehow managed to live in the hotel's cooling system despite the water's low temperature and high chlorine

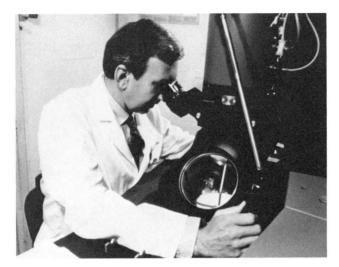

In order to spot the seemingly invisible legionella bacteria, McDade raised the microorganisms in protein-rich environments. After letting them grow, he viewed the bacteria with an electron microscope similar to the one used by this AIDS researcher.

content. Further research revealed that the bacteria were not new. They had caused mysterious outbreaks of pneumonialike sicknesses in 1965, 1968, and 1973. Several outbreaks followed the 1976 Philadelphia tragedy, including a 1981 incident in Windsor, Ontario, that hospitalized 395 people.

The discovery of the bacteria that cause Legionnaires' disease and an understanding of how these germs spread has enabled doctors to diagnose the illness on a routine basis. Each year, about 700 new cases of Legionnaires' disease are diagnosed and reported to U.S. medical authorities, who estimate that many thousands of cases probably remain unreported.

AIDS

In 1981, several rare and seemingly unrelated diseases were reported by doctors in different parts of the United States. In San Francisco, California, a physician examining a young homosexual man observed symptoms of a serious infection caused by a fungus and noted that the victim's immune system was not responding to fight the disease.

With his immune system malfunctioning, the young man became extremely susceptible to other types of infection and soon contracted

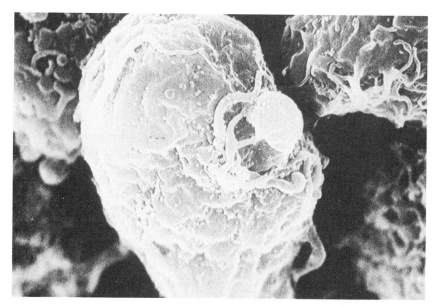

With its appearance in 1981, acquired immune deficiency syndrome (AIDS) challanged the first doctors who tried to diagnose it. As cases appeared nationwide, experts identified the disease by a shared symptom—its tendency to disturb the body's immune system. They did not produce a micrograph of the virus for several more years.

an unusual kind of pneumonia called *Pneumocystis carinii pneumonia*, or *PCP*. This disease, caused by a parasite, usually takes hold only in people whose immune system is impaired from lack of proper nutrition. Yet in this case the victim was not malnourished.

While the San Francisco doctor puzzled over the case, a physician in New York City also had some patients who were difficult to diagnose. Two young men, both gay, had developed *Kaposi's sarcoma,* or KS, a form of cancer rarely seen in the United States. Oddly, the KS in these two victims seemed to spread more quickly than in other recorded cases. Tests revealed that their immune systems were impaired, which allowed the disease to run wild through their bodies. Both doctors reported their findings to the CDC.

Within a few months, the CDC received more than 500 reports of cases of PCP and KS from around the country, all in gay men and all accompanied by a deficiency of the immune system. Concerned CDC doctors traveled from city to city, interviewing victims both inside and outside the local gay communities. The physicians hoped to uncover some clue, other than sexual preference, that would link all the victims.

Meanwhile, CDC labs tested samples of the patients' blood, urine, feces, and saliva but found no unusual microorganisms. Yet clearly something was attacking and destroying the victims' immune systems, leaving their bodies open to infection. Was the disease being spread through sexual contact? This seemed a strong possibility, considering that most of the victims belonged to a minority based on sexual preference.

By early 1982, similar cases began to appear among drug users who shared needles, as well as among people who had received blood transfusions. These victims were both male and female, and most were not gay. The medical investigators now had reason to believe that the new disease spread through contact with infected blood, either during sexual activity, drug use, or transfusions. Thus, the illness was not a disease of homosexuals, as some people had first thought.

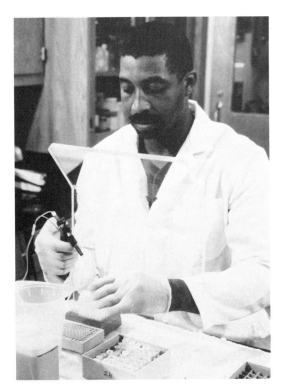

A CDC researcher performs a standard test, called the enzyme-linked immunosorbent assay (ELISA), to identify the presence of AIDS. Although these tests are highly accurate, they are usually double-checked when they show a positive result.

A technician is recording the results of a Western blot test. Because AIDS is so severe, this second test is run to ensure a correct diagnosis after ELISA procedures prove positive.

In the summer of 1982, doctors began to call the illness acquired immune deficiency syndrome and later shortened it to AIDS. As hundreds of new cases were reported in the United States and many other countries, the race was on to find the cause. In 1983, a research team led by Dr. Luc Montagnier in France isolated a virus, which was eventually identified as the cause of AIDS. Apparently, the virus attacks *T-cells*, white blood cells that form a major line of defense in the immune system. The virus then multiplies within these disease-fighting cells and eventually destroys them, crippling the immune system. An international committee of scientists later named the virus *human immunodeficiency virus*, or *HIV*.

In 1984, Dr. Robert Gallo of the National Institutes of Health in Maryland found a way to produce large quantities of HIV for study. Doctors were then able to develop a laboratory test that detects the virus in the blood. Although there is still no cure for AIDS, it is now possible for doctors to diagnose the disease with relatively high accuracy.

Physicians also know that, in addition to leaving the body open to other diseases, HIV sometimes creates its own symptoms. These can include extreme fatigue; swollen glands in the neck and armpits; unusual weight loss; a long-lasting, heavy cough; continual bouts of diarrhea; and bruises that form easily and last a long time. These symptoms and unusually severe infections or immune system problems alert doctors to the possible presence of AIDS.

CHRONIC FATIGUE SYNDROME

In 1984, an outbreak of a strange disease struck Incline Village, near Lake Tahoe, Nevada. Almost 200 of the town's 20,000 inhabitants displayed some or all of the same symptoms: sore throat, chills, fever, extreme fatigue, joint and muscle pain, memory loss, and troubled sleep. The symptoms were similar to those of *mononucleosis*, often called *mono*, a disease caused by the herpesvirus *Epstein-Barr*. But mono is usually found in children and teenagers, and the Lake Tahoe illness had struck many adults. It also seemed to last much longer than mono. After testing the patients, local doctors found no evidence of any known diseases, and CDC investigators were equally perplexed.

One of the first doctors to recognize that the disease was widespread was David Bell, a physician in Lyndonville, New York. In 1986, he read a news article about the Lake Tahoe outbreak and realized that many of his patients had begun reporting the same symptoms in 1985.

A CDC researcher processes an AIDS cell culture in a biosafety cabinet. These cultures will later be examined through an electron microscope.

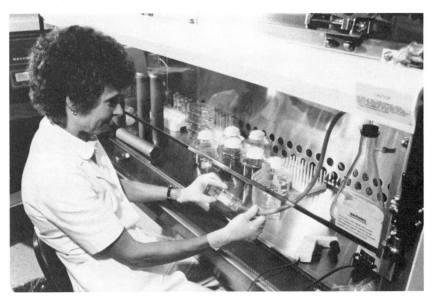

He had noticed the similarities to mono, but he also noted that some of the classic symptoms of mono were missing. Bell had performed every appropriate test but could not identify the illness. Reading about the Nevada outbreak, he realized that the cases he had encountered were not isolated. In fact, he soon learned, doctors all over the United States, as well as in Canada, England, Japan, and other countries, were reporting cases of the mysterious disease.

At first, Bell noticed that many doctors did not take the problem seriously. Unable to link the symptoms to specific, known diseases, many medical authorities dismissed the sufferers as *hypochondriacs*, healthy people who imagine they are ill. The problem was sarcastically labeled the "yuppie flu," because it typically affected young, middle-class people. But Bell and a number of other doctors realized that they were dealing with a real disease.

In 1987, a national conference on the illness was held in Portland, Oregon. There, Bell met many physicians who had tried to solve the riddle of the disease, including one of the doctors who had treated the Lake Tahoe patients. Although no consensus about the illness was reached at the conference, the meeting sent a signal to the medical community that the problem ought to be taken more seriously. In 1988, the CDC proposed that the disease seen by Bell and the others be named chronic fatigue syndrome, or CFS. No one as yet knows what causes CFS or how the disease is transmitted.

Because the illness is not widely recognized, some doctors continue to diagnose CFS symptoms as signs of other conditions. For example, sufferers often tend to act lethargic and listless, leading physicians to diagnose the problem as extreme depression. Dr. Paul Cheney, who has conducted important research on CFS, insists that the illness has nothing to do with depression. He states, "Depression requires a loss of interest in everything. These patients are just the opposite. They're terribly concerned about what their symptoms mean. They can't function. They can't work. Many are petrified. But they do not lack interest in their surroundings."

Until the cause of CFS is isolated and positively identified, diagnosis of this mystifying new disease will remain difficult and uncertain. This uncertainty constitutes a major health problem because CFS is widespread, and the number of cases appears to be growing steadily. The CDC and other medical organizations estimate that as many as 2 million to 5 million Americans suffer from the illness, whereas the number of sufferers worldwide may be in the tens of millions. Predicting that more and more attention will be focused on CFS in the next decade, Dr. Jay Levy, a California medical researcher, has called the problem "the disease of the '90s."

The occurrence of diseases such as Legionnaires', AIDS, and CFS illustrates that diagnosis, like other branches of medicine, is a constantly evolving discipline. As soon as doctors acquire new knowledge and develop techniques that enable them to identify and conquer one debilitating disease, another mystery ailment appears and creates new challenges. The final chapter looks at new, highly advanced technologies that doctors and scientists hope will meet some of these challenges to diagnosis.

CHAPTER 7
NEW DIAGNOSTIC TOOLS

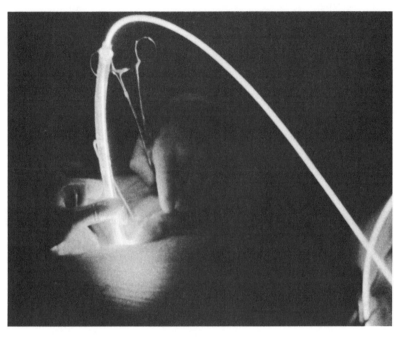

Recent diagnostic and treatment methods combine a variety of new technologies. Photodynamic therapy uses fiber optics and a laser to activate drugs that kill cancer cells.

The field of medical diagnosis and testing is constantly changing. Technology that is now considered state of the art, the most advanced available, eventually may become obsolete as new discoveries and inventions are incorporated into modern medical practice. The following examples demonstrate some of the more important advances in diagnostic science. Some researchers are developing technologies that are being used experimentally today and are expected to become routine during the next decade.

ADVANCES IN ENDOSCOPY

A large proportion of newly developed diagnostic tools and techniques are refinements of older methods. This type of progress is easily seen in the field of endoscopy. For example, the first scopes had to be nearly straight, because curves in the tubes blocked the doctor's view. But the 1970s brought *fiber optic* equipment made of transparent glass or plastic fibers designed to transmit light through internal reflections.

Fiber optics were first used in the field of communications. Information, including telephone communication, could be sent long distances via cables containing glass fibers. Beams of light carrying coded information moved through the fibers, and highly reflective surfaces inside the cables could carry the beams of information around curves. Medical researchers soon adapted this idea to endoscopy. Using fiber optics, the scopes inserted into the body were more flexible, moved longer distances, and afforded doctors brighter, clearer views.

Unlike ordinary light waves that scatter outward in many directions, laser light waves flow in a straight column. Thus, laser light is more intense and directed.

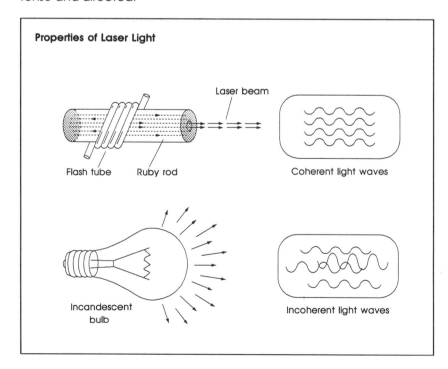

Even with fiber optics, however, the use of ordinary light in endoscopy has limitations. To fit inside blood vessels and other narrow spaces in the body, the tubes often must be extremely thin. This space allows a limited amount of light to shine in, and much of that light is absorbed by the lining of the tube itself. This problem has been overcome partially by the use of *lasers*, devices that emit a beam of extremely bright and concentrated light. Invented in the 1960s, lasers have since found thousands of applications in every branch of science.

Using laser light in endoscopy, doctors are constantly improving their ability to see the interior of the body. The unique nature and brightness of laser beams allow technicians to wire the scope's optical

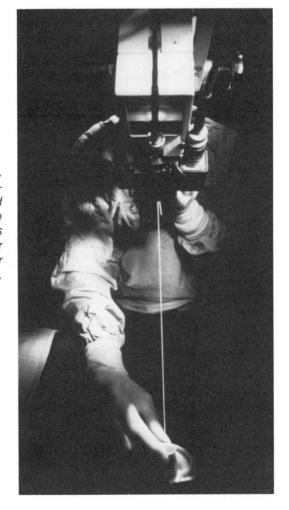

To make a diagnosis, physicians often combine fiber optics and laser light to view the interior of the body. This doctor is using fiber optics to guide a laser during ear surgery.

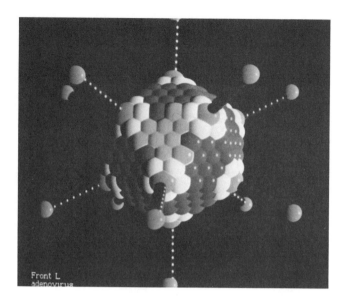

The technique of 3-D image processing combines microscopes, cameras, and computers to create three-dimensional images of individual cells. By looking closely at the body's intruders, such as this adenovirus, experts hope to identify and counteract the cause of illness.

fibers to television cameras. Thus, as the tube moves along inside the body, the fiber relays pictures to a screen. Videotape recordings allow the doctor to replay the images as often as necessary.

The laser also can be used to burn away malignant or damaged tissue during the endoscopic process itself. One new procedure, *laser angioplasty*, uses a laser beam in a fiber optic tube to burn away *plaque*, a fatty substance that often builds up on the insides of the arteries.

COMPUTERS AND THREE-DIMENSIONAL IMAGES

Another rapidly developing technology that promises to improve doctors' ability to visualize the body's interior is *3-D image processing*. This method combines three technological tools—the microscope, the camera, and the computer—to create three-dimensional images of individual human cells. Although it is still highly experimental, the technique has already produced impressive results.

In 1990, Steven Young and Mark Ellisman, two doctors from the University of California at San Diego School of Medicine, used 3-D imaging to produce remarkable pictures of brain cells from patients afflicted with *Alzheimer's disease*. This serious illness, which primarily attacks elderly people, is characterized by confusion, forgetfulness, and brain deterioration.

The two researchers collected samples of brain tissue from Alzheimer's patients, then used laser beams to slice the samples into sheets only one-hundred-thousandth of an inch thick. They placed the sheets, one at a time, under an electron microscope. They repeatedly focused on one particular cell, taking a microphotograph of each sheet. The cell was 400 "sheets" thick, producing 400 photos, each of a different layer of the cell.

Ellisman and Young converted the photo images into electronic signals that a computer used to produce a three-dimensional image of the whole cell. In a *Discover* magazine article (July 1990), Ellisman explained, "The computer allows us to rotate and magnify a three-dimensional cell and view its components from different perspectives. In this way, we can better understand how different intracellular

Positron emission tomography (PET scan) is a new technology that is especially useful for measuring the movement of fluid throughout the body over a prolonged period.

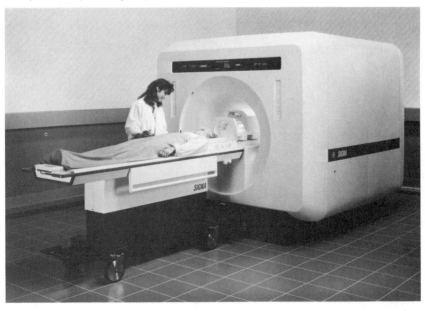

structures are related to one another. . . . We're trying to establish a whole gallery of cells representing different stages in the disease process." The researchers believe that doctors will be able to use this technique to diagnose problems by viewing diseased cells directly.

NEW SCANNING TECHNIQUES

For years doctors have used such tests as the EKG and angiogram to find out whether the insides of the arteries are clear of plaque. When much plaque is present, blood flow is restricted, the heart cannot perform its job properly, and the chances for heart disease and heart attack increase. The EKG is often a valuable tool, but it can miss evidence of heart disease as often as 30% of the time. Angiograms involve inserting tubes into the body, a procedure that carries a small risk of disturbing the heart's rhythm and killing the patient. The test is also expensive, costing as much as $5,000.

Positron emission tomography, also called the *PET scan*, is a technique that was first used experimentally in the 1980s. It is beginning to provide doctors with information about heart disease that is more accurate than an EKG and less expensive and risky than an angiogram. In a PET-scan procedure, the patient is injected with a substance that emits tiny particles called *positrons* (positively charged

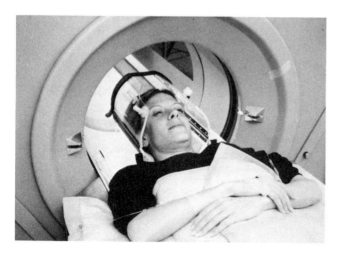

PET scans are administered by placing the patient inside a machine with a huge magnet that causes the body's electrical charges to align with it. When the magnet is turned off, the machine maps the body's changes as it returns to its usual state.

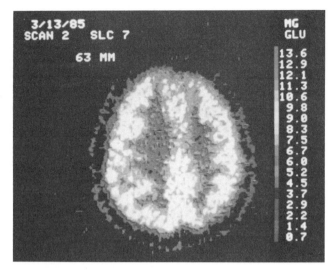

A PET scan enables experts to see an area of the body from every angle. This image shows one layer of a healthy human brain.

electrons). The patient lies down for one to two hours, allowing the substance to circulate through the body and reach the heart and other organs. As the substance travels, a special device that detects positrons records the motions of the heart and other organs from various angles. A computer then analyzes the information and produces brightly colored computerized images.

According to science writer Avery Comatrow, studies show that "PET scans are extraordinarily accurate and sensitive, yet cost no more than other tests that perform less well." Nevertheless, the method is not yet widespread. The necessary equipment requires an expensive initial investment, so few hospitals and medical centers in the United States currently have PET scanners. Those with the equipment offer PET scans for about $1,500. Perhaps the PET-scan procedure's greatest advantage is its low level of risk; no cutting or insertion of tubes is required.

READING LIFE'S BLUEPRINTS

One of the most revolutionary and controversial medical technologies to emerge in the last two decades is *genetic testing*. Although scientists have just begun to develop techniques in this field, the research has already had a profound impact on the field of diagnosis, as well as on such diverse areas as prenatal care, hospital care of newborns, and health care insurance.

Genetic testing is based on the rapidly expanding body of knowledge about *genes*, tiny chemical units strung together in strands called *chromosomes* and found in the nucleus of the body's cells. Scientists estimate that each cell contains about 100,000 genes, which constitute a complete set of instructions, or a sort of microscopic blueprint, for constructing a human being. These genetic blueprints are formed by a combination of a mother's and father's genes that are passed along to their offspring.

Some genes are defective, leading to mistakes in the body's blueprint that result in disease or deformity. One or two defective genes located in a specific spot on a specific chromosome can cause an inherited disorder. By locating and identifying these specific defective genes, scientists can develop tests that diagnose many diseases and disorders.

So far, only about 2,000, or 2%, of human genes have been located, and many sites are only approximations. But genetic technology is

Drs. Helen Donis-Keller and Philip Green are researchers for a federal project that plans to map the strings of genes found in all humans. Genes contain the physiological instructions that each person inherits at birth.

improving yearly. Scientists recently isolated the genes involved in juvenile diabetes, rheumatoid arthritis, cystic fibrosis, and a number of other disorders. The National Institutes of Health and the U.S. Department of Energy recently began a multibillion-dollar 15-year project to locate and identify every human gene.

Tests already can be administered to babies in the womb to detect and predict problems such as *Down's syndrome,* which is caused by a chromosomal abnormality and is characterized by moderate to severe mental retardation; *phenylketonuria* (PKU), a liver problem that leads to mental retardation; *hemophilia,* a blood disease; *muscular dystrophy*, which causes wasting of the muscles; and more than 300 other disorders and conditions. Parents who learn that their child will be born with a crippling or life-threatening problem sometimes choose to end the pregnancy by abortion.

Genetic diagnostic testing does not end with a child's birth. Most states now have laws that require testing of newborns for up to nine inherited disorders. Early detection of some disorders can lead to effective treatment that enables the child to live a relatively normal life. For instance, babies with PKU can be put on a special diet that prevents mental retardation.

Like any new technology, however, genetic testing has the potential for misuse. Some large businesses are already using it on prospective employees to detect physical problems that have not yet appeared but may occur later in life. The employers worry that some of the workers they hire might develop diseases and disorders that will increase the company's health care insurance premiums. Some job applicants have complained that they were refused employment on the basis of these genetic tests.

Some activists, such as sociologist Dorothy Nelkin and attorney Lawrence Tancredi, call this practice "genetic discrimination." If the practice becomes widespread, they say, people with such common problems as diabetes and epilepsy may not be able to find work. Nelkin and Tancredi warn, "We risk increasing the number of people defined as unemployable, untrainable, or uninsurable. We risk creating a biologic underclass." Many experts say that laws prohibiting genetic discrimination eventually may need to be enacted.

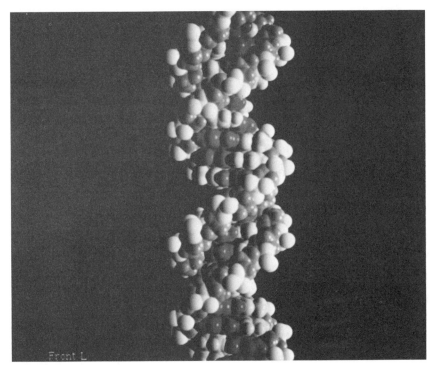

A model of DNA (genetic material). A recent form of diagnosis involves genetic testing. By looking at models of DNA strands, scientists are learning to identify inherited diseases early in a person's life.

Proponents of genetic testing say that, despite any social problems the technology may create initially, the technique promises to open new medical vistas and to become a powerful diagnostic tool. They point out that increased genetic research may allow scientists eventually to conquer cancer, heart disease, diabetes, and a host of other problems.

Each new leap in medical technology leads to further advances and improvements in a doctor's ability to diagnose disease. Less than 200 years ago, the simple stethoscope was considered a medical marvel. Today, computerized scanners probe the cells of the heart and brain in an effort to unlock their secrets. What will the next 200 years bring? By the time that question is answered, today's greatest scientific advances may be relics of idle curiosity resting in museum showcases.

APPENDIX:
FOR MORE INFORMATION

The following is a list of organizations that can provide further information about many of the topics included in this book.

GENERAL INFORMATION

Centers for Disease Control
1600 Clifton Road, NE
Atlanta, GA 30333
(404) 639-3311

Massachusetts General Hospital
32 Fruit Street
Boston, MA 02114
(617) 726-2000

National Institute of Allergy and Infectious Diseases
Department of Health and Human Services
National Institutes of Health
Building 31, Room 7A32
Bethesda, MD 20892
(301) 496-5717

National Organization for Rare Disorders (information clearinghouse)
P.O. Box 8923
New Fairfield, CT 06812-1783
(203) 746-6518 (in Connecticut)
(800) 447-6673 (outside Connecticut)

University of California Medical Center
10833 Le Conte Avenue
Los Angeles, CA 90024
(213) 825-9111

University of Chicago Medical Center
5841 Maryland Avenue
Chicago, IL 60637
(312) 702-1000

AIDS

AIDS Action Council
2033 M Street NW, Suite 802
Washington, DC 20036
(202) 293-2886

Canadian Foundation for AIDS Research
120 Bloor Street East
First Floor
Toronto, ON M4W 1B8
Canada
(416) 972-6281

National AIDS Hotline
(800) 342-AIDS

National HIV and AIDS Information Service
Public Health Service General Information Hot Line
(800) 342-2437

CANCER

American Cancer Society
1599 Clifton Road, NE
Atlanta, GA 30329
(800) ACS-2345

Canadian Cancer Society
10 Alcorn Avenue, Suite 200
Toronto, ON M4V 3B1
Canada
(416) 961-7223

Memorial Sloan-Kettering Cancer Center
1275 York Avenue
New York, NY 10021
(212) 639-2000

DIABETES

American Diabetes Association
1660 Duke Street
Alexandria, VA 22314
(703) 549-1500 (in Virginia)
(800) 232-3472 (outside Virginia)

Canadian Diabetes Association
78 Bond Street
Toronto, ON M5B 2J8
Canada
(416) 362-4440

Juvenile Diabetes Foundation International
60 Madison Avenue
New York, NY 10010

(212) 889-7575 (in New York)
(800) 533-2873

The National Diabetes Information Clearinghouse
Box NDIC
9000 Rockville Pike
Bethesda, MD 20892
(301) 468-2162

HEART DISEASE

American Heart Association
7220 Greenville Avenue
Dallas, TX 75231
(214) 373-6300

Canadian Cardiovascular Society
360 Victoria Avenue, Room 401
Westmount, PQ H3Z 2N4
Canada
(514) 482-3407

The Coronary Club, Inc.
Cleveland Clinic Educational Foundation
9500 Euclid Avenue, Room E4-15
Cleveland, OH 44195
(216) 444-3690

Heart and Stroke Foundation of Canada
160 George Street, Suite 200
Ottawa, ON K1N 9M2
Canada
(613) 237-4361

National Heart, Lung, and Blood Institute
National Institutes of Health
9000 Rockville Pike
Building 31, Room 4A21
Bethesda, MD 20892
(301) 496-4236

FURTHER READING

GENERAL INFORMATION

Ackertnecht, Erwin. *A Short History of Medicine.* Baltimore: Johns Hopkins University Press, 1982.

Alcamo, I. Edward. *Fundamentals of Microbiology.* Reading, MA: Addison-Wesley, 1983.

Brenner, Zara R. *Diagnostic Tests and Procedures.* East Norwalk, CT: Appleton & Lange, 1987.

Brownlee, Shannon. "The Assurances of Genes." *U.S. News & World Report* (July 23, 1990).

Comatrow, Avery. "One Man, Pummeled by Positrons." *U.S. News & World Report* (August 6, 1990).

Dean, Herbert, M. *Look to Your Health.* New York: Van Nostrand Reinhold, 1980.

Ferguson, Lewis. *Explain It to Me Doctor.* Philadelphia: Lippincott, 1970.

Hensel, Bruce. *Smart Medicine: How to Get the Most out of Your Medical Checkup and Stay Healthy.* New York: Putnam, 1989.

Hudson, Robert P. *Disease and Its Control: The Shaping of Modern Thought.* Westport, CT: Greenwood Press, 1983.

Lyons, Albert. *Medicine: An Illustrated History*. New York: Abradale Press, 1987.

Malasanos, Lois, Violet Barkauskas, and Kathryn Stoltenberg-Allen. *Health Assessment*. 4th ed. St. Louis: Mosby, 1990.

Moskowitz, Mark A., and Michael E. Osband. *The Complete Book of Medical Tests*. New York: Norton, 1984.

Nardo, Don. *Lasers: Humanity's Magic Light*. San Diego: Lucent Books, 1990.

Panati, Charles. *Breakthroughs: Astonishing Advances in Your Lifetime in Medicine, Science, and Technology*. Boston: Houghton Mifflin, 1980.

Rossman, I. J., and Doris R. Schwartz. *The Family Handbook of Home Nursing and Medical Care*. New York: Evans, 1968.

AIDS

Cantwell, Alan. *AIDS: The Mystery and the Solution*. Los Angeles: Aries Rising, 1986.

Hyde, Margaret O., and Elizabeth H. Forsyth. *AIDS: What Does It Mean to You?* New York: Walker, 1986.

LeVert, Suzanne. *AIDS: In Search of a Killer*. Englewood Cliffs, NJ: Messner, 1987.

Madaras, Lynda. *Lynda Madaras Talks to Teens About AIDS: An Essential Guide for Parents, Teachers, and Young People*. New York: Newmarket, 1988.

Silverstein, Alvin, and Virginia B. Silverstein. *AIDS: Deadly Threat*. Hillside, NJ: Enslow, 1988.

CANCER

Anku, Vincent. *What to Know About the Treatment of Cancer.* Seattle: Madrona, 1984.

Dreher, Henry. *Your Defense Against Cancer: The Complete Guide to Cancer Prevention.* New York: HarperCollins, 1989.

Kothari, M. L., and L. A. Mehta. *Cancer: Myths and Realities of Cause and Cure.* New York: Boyars, 1979.

Le Shan, Lawrence. *Cancer as a Turning Point: A Handbook for People with Cancer, Their Families, and Health Professionals.* New York: Dutton, 1989.

CHRONIC FATIGUE SYNDROME

Cowley, Geoffrey. "Chronic Fatigue Syndrome: A Modern Medical Mystery." *Newsweek* (November 12, 1990).

DIABETES

Bloom, A. *Diabetes Explained.* Norwell, MA: Kluwer Academic, 1982.

Brown, Joseph F. *Diabetes Dictionary and Guide.* Maryland Heights, MO: Press West, 1978.

Duncan, Theodore G. *The Diabetes Fact Book.* New York: Scribners, 1983.

MacLean, Heather, and Barbara Oram. *Living with Diabetes.* Cheektowaga, NY: University of Toronto Press, 1988.

Silverstein, Alvin, and Virginia B. Silverstein. *Diabetes: The Sugar Disease.* New York: HarperCollins: 1980.

HEART DISEASE

The American Medical Association Book of Heartcare. New York: Random House, 1982.

Crockett, James E. *Your Heart: In Sickness and in Health.* Kansas City: Eucalyptus Press, 1984.

Silverstein, Alvin, and Virginia B. Silverstein. *Heart Disease: America's Number One Killer.* New York: HarperCollins, 1985.

Ward, Brian. *The Heart and Blood.* New York: Watts, 1982.

INFLUENZA

Dowdle, Walter, and Jack La Patra. *Informed Consent: Influenza Facts and Myths.* Chicago: Nelson-Hall, 1983.

Osborn, June, ed. *Influenza in America 1918–1976: History, Science, and Politics.* Canton, MA: Watson, 1977.

Prevention Magazine Editors. *Stopping Sickness.* Edited by Sharon Faelton. Emmaus, PA: Rodale Press, 1987.

Stedman, Nancy. *The Common Cold and Influenza.* Englewood Cliffs, NJ: Messner, 1987.

Tortora, Gerard J., et al. *Microbiology: An Introduction.* New York: Benjamin/Cummings, 1989.

GLOSSARY

AIDS acquired immune deficiency syndrome; an acquired defect in the immune system; the final stage of the disease caused by the human immunodeficiency virus (HIV); spread through the blood, sexual contact, nutritive fluids passed from a mother to her fetus, or breast milk; leaves victims vulnerable to certain, often fatal, infections and cancers

angiogram a series of X rays taken to view blood vessels after they are injected with a special dye that is impenetrable to X rays

arthroscopy a type of endoscopy used to examine the joints between the bones

basal metabolism test a diagnostic exam that determines how much oxygen a person consumes when he or she is at digestive, physical, and emotional rest

benign harmless

biopsy a test in which body tissue samples are removed and examined under a microscope to diagnose types of cancer

bronchoscopy a type of endoscopy used to examine the bronchi, the main branches of the trachea that lead to the lungs

bubonic plague plague; a rare disease, caused by bacteria, that affects the lymph nodes and releases toxins into the circulatory system

chromosomes rodlike structures containing genetic material and protein found in the nuclei of cells

chronic fatigue syndrome CFS; a disease similar to mononucleosis, characterized by sore throat, chills, fever, extreme fatigue, and joint and muscle pain; CFS has been diagnosed only recently and no cure has yet been found

computerized axial tomography CT scan; an advanced type of X-ray process that uses a scanner to take pictures from several different directions, thus producing a three-dimensional image; CT scans are especially useful in diagnosing brain abnormalities

culture a test in which a physician grows microorganisms in a special environment to detect the presence of infection

diabetes a disease, characterized by frequent urination, excessive thirst, and fatigue, caused by an accumulation of glucose (natural sugar) in the bloodstream

diagnosis the identification of a disease or medical problem from its signs or symptoms

dipstick analysis a urine-testing procedure using chemical-coated strips of plastic that change color when they react with various substances in urine

dyspnea difficult or labored breathing

electrocardiogram EKG; the tracing produced by an electrocardiograph

electrocardiograph a machine used to diagnose heart disease by charting and detecting heart muscle contractions

electroencephalogram EEG; a recording of electrical activity in the brain; electrodes attached to the head produce graphs of electrical brain activity on a computer screen or printout

emboli abnormal particles, such as air bubbles or blood clots, obstructing the blood vessels

endemic restricted to a particular area

endoscopy an examination of the body's organs and cavities using an endoscope, a flexible tube with an attached light source that is inserted through an opening in the body

epidemic a highly contagious disease that spreads rapidly, affecting many people within a population or community

fiber optics thin, transparent, flexible fibers of glass or plastic that transmit light by reflecting it off the side of fibers; used in endoscopic examinations

fluoroscopy a procedure in which physicians implant substances opaque to X rays into the human body and can then observe the internal structure of the body by following the flow of those substances using an image projected onto a fluorescent screen

gastroscope an instrument for inspecting the interior of the stomach

genes tiny, complex units of chemical material contained within the chromosomes; variations in the patterns formed by the components of genes are responsible for inherited traits

genetic testing methods by which doctors can identify a disease or disorder by locating defective genes

glucose tolerance test a lab procedure that measures levels of sugar in the blood

history an account of a patient's personal background, past and present health, and all illnesses suffered by his or her relatives

influenza a highly contagious disease characterized by an infection of the lungs and upper respiratory tract, high fever, chills, and severe cough

inspection the first step in a medical examination, during which the physician takes the patient's pulse and inspects the external parts of the body to make a diagnosis

laparoscopy a type of endoscopy that examines the uterus and other abdominal organs

laser an acronym for light amplification by stimulated emission of radiation; an instrument used in diagnosis that emits a bright and concentrated beam of light into the body; used to produce an image that can then be transmitted onto a television screen for viewing

Legionnaire's disease a severe, often fatal disease caused by the presence of the legionella bacteria and characterized by high fever, dry cough, chills, headache, weakness, and fatigue

malignant harmful; cancerous

mammogram an X ray of the breasts that is used to detect breast cancer

microbiology the study of microorganisms

ophthalmoscope an instrument for viewing the interior of the eye

palpation the second step in a doctor's examination, in which he or she looks for abnormalities by feeling parts of the body for swelling, pain, tenderness, or broken bones

Pap smear a test used to detect early signs of uterine cancer

percussion the third step in an examination, wherein the doctor taps on certain parts of the body, often while listening through a stethoscope; this technique can help determine the presence of fluid in the lungs and the size of the heart, liver, stomach, and spleen

positron emission tomography PET scan; a procedure wherein positively charged electrons injected into a patient enter the bloodstream and travel throughout the body, become absorbed by specific organs, and are detected by a special device that records the flow of blood and motions of the organ

prognosis prediction of the course of a disease and how long it will persist

sign objective evidence of a disease that, unlike a symptom, may not be evident to a patient but is observed and interpreted by a physician

stethoscope an instrument used to detect and magnify sounds produced in the body

streptococci a type of bacteria

symptom obvious evidence of a disease, often signaling to a patient that he or she is ill

3-D image processing a procedure that creates a three-dimensional picture of an individual body cell

trachea windpipe; the main trunk of a system of tubes, about four inches long and an inch in diameter, that passes air to and from the lungs

X ray a shadowy picture of internal parts of the body, produced by passing radiation through the body and registering the resulting image on sensitive photographic material

INDEX

PICTURE CREDITS

Don Nardo is a writer, actor, filmmaker, and composer. He has written articles, short stories, and more than 20 books, as well as screenplays and teleplays, including work for Warner Bros. and ABC television. He has appeared in dozens of stage productions and has worked in front of or behind the camera in 20 films. His musical compositions, such as his oratorio *Richard III* and his film score for a version of *The Time Machine,* have been played by regional orchestras. Mr. Nardo lives with his wife on Cape Cod, Massachusetts.

Dale C. Garell, M.D., is medical director of California Children Services, Department of Health Services, County of Los Angeles. He is also associate dean for curriculum at the University of Southern California School of Medicine and clinical professor in the Department of Pediatrics & Family Medicine at the University of Southern California School of Medicine. From 1963 to 1974, he was medical director of the Division of Adolescent Medicine at Children's Hospital in Los Angeles. Dr. Garell has served as president of the Society for Adolescent Medicine, chairman of the youth committee of the American Academy of Pediatrics, and as a forum member of the White House Conference on Children (1970) and White House Conference on Youth (1971). He has also been a member of the editorial board of the *American Journal of Diseases of Children.*

C. Everett Koop, M.D., Sc.D., is former Surgeon General, deputy assistant secretary for health, and director of the Office of International Health of the U.S. Public Health Service. A pediatric surgeon with an international reputation, he was previously surgeon-in-chief of Children's Hospital of Philadelphia and professor of pediatric surgery and pediatrics at the University of Pennsylvania. Dr. Koop is the author of more than 175 articles and books on the practice of medicine. He has served as surgery editor of the *Journal of Clinical Pediatrics* and editor-in-chief of the *Journal of Pediatric Surgery.* Dr. Koop has received nine honorary degrees and numerous other awards, including the Denis Brown Gold Medal of the British Association of Paediatric Surgeons, the William E. Ladd Gold Medal of the American Academy of Pediatrics, and the Copernicus Medal of the Surgical Society of Poland. He is a chevalier of the French Legion of Honor and a member of the Royal College of Surgeons, London.